Breads from Betsy's Kitchen

BETSY OPPENNEER

Edited by Mark Oppenneer

Published by The Breadworks, Inc.
RR1 Box 238A
Canaan, NH 03741

First Edition
     Second Printing

Written and designed by Betsy Oppenneer
Edited by Mark Oppenneer
Cover designed by Dick Lyons

Library of Congress Catalog Card Number: 98-92808

Oppenneer, Betsy.
     Breads from Betsy's Kitchen/Betsy Oppenneer. – 1st ed.
     Includes index.
     ISBN 0-9627665-4-2
     1. Bread   1. Title

Printed in the USA by

WIMMER
The Wimmer Companies
Memphis
1-800-548-2537

Contents

Acknowledgements 7

Foreword 9

Welcome to My Kitchen 12

Utensils, Ingredients & Techniques 12

Loaves & Baguettes.. 28

Rolls, Bagels & Buns 100

Specialty Breads.. 124

Sweet Breads 154

Trouble Shooting.. 180

Sources 182

Index... 184

A Word of Welcome...

I started baking when I was 8-years old, doing projects for Brownie Scout merit badges. By age 12, I was working at a local bakery. I must have gotten flour in my veins because cooking and baking have always been my passion, especially bread baking. Baking bread is one of the most satisfying experiences in life. I love to see others getting as excited about baking as I am.

This book has many of the recipes from my first book, **Betsy's Breads**. After selling over 15,000 copies, we made the decision to remove it from print. Since many of those recipes were my favorites, I decided to update them and put them in this book along with many others that have evolved over the eleven years since that book was written.

I've tried to make this book as easy to read as possible. For example, ingredients marked as "divided" are used more than once in a recipe. When this is the case, each instance of the divided ingredient is written in italics. Throughout the book you'll also find boxes titled "Bits & Pieces." These boxes contain history, tips, techniques, and trivia. I hope this will add even more enjoyment to your reading.

So, as you can see, **Breads from Betsy's Kitchen** is not only filled with good information, scrumptious recipes, history, and trivia, it's filled with love, too! Bon Appetit...

Betsy Oppenneer

Acknowledgements

I WOULD LIKE TO THANK:

- My son, Mark, for the work and effort he has put into this project as editor. We've always worked well together, and writing this book was even more special since we created together. He worked on the text while attending the University at Albany (SUNY) for his Master's in English Education. I consider him one of the best wordsmiths I have ever encountered. He's been every bit as much of a taskmaster as my editor was on my last book with a major publisher!

- My good friend, Dick Lyons, from Washington State for his beautiful cover art. We've always looked forward to receiving Dick's hand-painted Christmas cards each year – you can see why! I absolutely love his picture and feel it invites you right into my kitchen!

- My mother, Alice Wright, for her proofreading skills. She's an ex-bookkeeper and a stickler for detail. She's also one of my biggest supporters and I definitely could not have done this book without her.

- My son, Erik, for his proofreading skills. He has always been an encouragement and inspiration to me. His sense of humor keeps me from bogging down when I get carried away with my projects.

- And last, but definitely not least, my husband, Keith, for being my most loyal fan, my most discriminating tester and my most vocal critic (in a good way!). He's tasted the good and bad. I know I can always count on him to be completely honest.

Foreword

How fitting that I should write the Foreword to my Mom's book. Although I am not a loaf of bread, I am largely a product of Betsy's kitchen (and I mean largely!). For the first eighteen years of my life, I ate a strict diet consisting of Betsy's four food groups: sweet, savory, sourdough, and specialty breads. If it's true that "you are what you eat," then I am a living testament to the incredible recipes in this volume: I am often bold and zesty, sometimes crusty, and certainly soft on the inside.

As I edited this text, so many memories flitted through my mind...mornings when the powerful aroma of fresh warm bread would lure me, half-awake, into the kitchen; coming home from school to a kitchen alive with activity as Mom, hands covered with flour, worked her magic. I remembered sneaking downstairs for a late night snack of leftover dinner rolls; stealing sweet cookie dough from the mixing bowl when Mom wasn't looking - so many wonderful recollections of my youth, and all of them revolving around Betsy's kitchen.

Working with my Mom on this book has been a pleasure and an honor. What a rare opportunity - to work on a project that involves three of my greatest loves: my Mom, her baking, and language. Over the last couple of months, I have seen **Breads From Betsy's Kitchen** grow from a handful of "old faithfuls" into an astounding resource for the home baker. This book has become more than just a collection of recipes. It is a reflection of my Mom's tireless devotion to sharing the joys of bread baking with others.

I am proud to be a part of her creative vision. For the last two decades, Betsy has traveled the world spreading the gospel of bread baking at cooking schools, stores, charity events, and private homes. And now, with this volume, you get a slice of that pie - a small piece of her love for baking. As these recipes become breads from your kitchen, I wish you the same joy they have given me and my family. Enjoy!

Mark Oppenneer

Utensils
Ingredients
Tips & Techniques

Welcome to My Bread Baker's Kitchen

When I step into my kitchen to bake a bread recipe, I never know exactly how the loaves will turn out. So many things affect the outcome of the baking process. For instance, the weather, altitude, freshness of ingredients - and the way you measure them - can make the same recipe produce different results. Fortunately, there are ways to achieve certainty in the kitchen. The simplest way is making sure you have the right utensils and equipment. The utensils in my kitchen fall into two categories: necessities and luxuries. In some cases, the line separating these categories is very thin. Let's take a quick look around and I'll show you the utensils I find useful for bread baking.

UTENSILS

BAKING PANS AND SHEETS. I use heavyweight dull-to-dark baking pans. Shiny pans reflect the heat rays of the oven and prevent breads from browning properly. This also happens with the cushioned-air pans (I avoid using this type of pan always). Lightweight pans do not conduct heat well and prevent bread from baking evenly.

Two recipes in the book call for special pans, brioche and gugelhopf. The brioche pan is a fluted pan that looks like a large flat-bottomed coffee filter. You can use an 8-inch soufflé dish or other round casserole in its place. For the gugelhopf (a tube pan with fancy sides) you can substitute a 10" bundt pan.

BAKING STONE. Stones gather heat which helps produce crisp crusts during baking. Although I recommend them, I have to admit that good stones are not cheap. I prefer a stone 14 by 16 inches and 5/8 of an inch thick because I can bake multiple loaves and rolls at once on it. When your stone becomes stained, clean it in a self-cleaning oven.

EIGHT-INCH WHISK. I use whisks made by Best Manufacturers in Portland, Oregon. They last a long time and are sealed so that liquid won't work its way up into the handle. Because the whisks are long and thin, they fit into measuring cups and the corners of saucepans. I use this whisk to dissolve yeast (did you know that yeast will dissolve instantly with a whisk, but will stick to other utensils?), beat eggs in cups, and to beat powdered sugar with liquids for a smooth icing or glaze.

HEAVY-DUTY ROUX WHISK OR DANISH DOUGH WHISK. These whisks both have strong thick wires, which make them great for mixing heavy dough. The Roux whisk is available in most cookware stores and catalogues. The Danish Dough whisk is not always easy to find in stores. Unlike wooden spoons, these whisks don't absorb moisture or carry germs. Using a regular whisk to mix dough often results in a goopy mess (the dough gets inside the wires and forms a ball).

INSTANT-READ THERMOMETER. Although many people have a good feel for the temperature of the liquids that go into a recipe, an instant-read thermometer never lies! It lets you know the exact temperature of the liquid in your recipe so you get the most out of your yeast. Using an instant-read thermometer is also a foolproof way to tell if your bread is done: just stick it into the loaf ~ when it registers 190 degrees, your bread is ready.

LARGE CERAMIC BOWL (four to six-quart capacity). Ceramic bowls hold heat and give a wonderful "incubating" warmth to rising dough (heat the bowl first by filling it with lukewarm water). I prefer bowls with straighter, less-rounded sides. These allow less air to reach the surface of my dough when it's rising.

LARGE WIRE RACK. A wire rack is one of the most essential items for the serious bread baker (you should have at least one, if not two!). As soon as bread comes out of the oven, it should be removed from its pan and placed on a rack. This allows air to circulate freely and keeps the bread from sweating which will make it soggy.

LONG-BLADED SCISSORS. These are handy for cutting dough when making wreaths, snipping tops of rolls or loaves, and cutting pizza. I also prefer using scissors instead of a knife when cutting up dried fruits.

MEASURING CUPS (both liquid and dry). Didn't know there are two kinds of measuring cups? Liquid cups have a pour spout, whereas dry cups are flat so you can swipe across the rim for more accurate measuring.

MEASURING SPOONS. I use long-handled spoons with long narrow bowls. These kind fit through the small mouths of spice jars easier than round-bowled spoons do.

PASTRY BRUSHES. These are handy for brushing glazes on breads. When I want to remove excess flour from dough during the rolling process, they serve as little brooms.

PLASTIC DOUGH SCRAPER AND/OR METAL BENCH SCRAPER. I have both kinds of scrapers and each serves a different purpose. I usually use the plastic scraper to clean a bowl and to scrape the film that develops on my work surface when I'm kneading dough. I knead on a wooden surface and plastic doesn't gouge it when I'm really "going to town." I use a metal scraper to divide dough.

PROFESSIONAL PARCHMENT PAPER. I do most of my baking on parchment paper. It's easy to clean up and it gives my breads a softer bottom crust (keeps breads with sugar in them from caramelizing on the bottom like they do on baking sheets). Professional parchment paper can be used in ovens heated up to 425 degrees. Less expensive brands of parchment become brittle and shatter if they are placed in ovens over 375 degrees and cannot be reused. I use one sheet of professional parchment several times unless I'm making something particularly messy. Parchment paper is also good for moving risen dough onto a baking stone. Shape the dough on parchment then slip the paper and all onto your preheated stone. You get the same benefits of baking with a stone without all the hassle and mess of trying to slide the dough off a paddle.

ROLLING PIN. I use a 16 to 18-inch, heavyweight, solid-cylinder rolling pin. The one I use most often doesn't have handles. By rolling the pin with my hands in the center rather than on the sides (using the pin's handles), the thickness of my dough is more uniform. I season and clean my hardwood rolling pins with vegetable oil so they won't stick to my dough.

SERRATED KNIVES. Serrated knives make slicing your finished loaves an easy task. My favorite knives are made by Wüstoff-Trident because they hold an edge better than any other knives I've used. I especially like their Konditormesser Super Slicer with a thick 10-inch-long serrated blade that is perfect for slicing crisp-crusted artesian and European-style breads. I also use the Wüstoff-Trident's 5-inch serrated tomato knife. Yes, it's great for slicing tomatoes, but I use it to slit the tops of loaves before baking. Over the years I've bought special expensive slicers, razorblades, and cutters, but nothing does as well as a short-bladed, sharp serrated knife. I've cut a whole tray of rolls with this knife without having to stop and clean the blade like I would have to do with other knives or blades.

TIGHTLY WOVEN TOWELS OR PLASTIC WRAP. These are great for covering dough as it rises; both keep the air out. I use towels since they can be re-used (with the amount of baking I do, I can't afford to throw away all that plastic wrap!). Tightly woven towels, such as linen or flour sacks, work best. Terry-type and loosely woven towels allow too much air to reach the dough.

TIMER. I use a battery operated triple-timer so that I can keep track of many things at one time. They time as far out as 10 hours, which makes them much more convenient than standard 1-hour timers.

I could add many other items to the list above, but these are the bread baking essentials. One item I did not add to this list, but use frequently, is a heavy-duty mixer. When I have the time, I love getting my hands into the dough. When I'm in a rush, the mixer is invaluable. You can make the recipes in this book by hand or with a mixer.

Another way to achieve certainty in the kitchen is to understand the qualities and characteristics of the ingredients you use. We all know that sugar is sweet and water is wet, but ingredients react with others in some ways you can't see, feel, or smell. Knowing how they react is one of the best ways to ensure a successful loaf. Let's head to the pantry and refrigerator for a closer look...

INGREDIENTS

YEAST. Yeast is amazing. The small yeast granules are actually living fungi that, in a way, hibernate until contact with warm water activates them. In bread, yeast feeds on the natural sugars in the flour and creates carbon dioxide gas. The gas fills the gluten meshwork formed by the kneading process, which in turn makes the bread rise. Yeast is commercially available in three forms:

Active Dry Yeast. You can buy active dry yeast in small foil packages or in jars at the grocery store. You can also get it in bulk at some specialty food stores (if you buy bulk, use one scant tablespoon of yeast for each package of active dry yeast called for in a recipe).

Compressed or Fresh Yeast. Compressed, or fresh, yeast is available at grocery or health food stores (in the refrigerated section), and from some bakeries. Fresh yeast requires more effort to use than the other kinds - it takes longer to prepare, doesn't last as long in storage, and won't hold up well in the freezer - but, it produces breads with a wonderfully intense flavor and a smooth texture.

Fast-Rising* or *Quick-Rising Yeast. You can cut the
dough's rising time in half by substituting quick-rising
yeast for the yeast in any recipe. I get the best results by
preparing this type of yeast with the rapid mix method
(combine the undissolved yeast with three-fourths of the
flour and the other dry ingredients, then add the liquid at
a temperature of 120 to 130 degrees).

FLOUR. As I mentioned above, the natural sugars in flour feed
the yeast. Flour gives yeast a "carbo-boost," much like the lift
humans get from sugar. But flour serves another purpose:
when mixed with liquids and agitated, it forms a gluten
meshwork that gives bread its structure. For this reason, it is
important to use hard wheat flour – not soft wheat flour –
when making yeast breads. Soft wheat flour does not contain
enough protein to form gluten, which means that your bread
won't rise very high. Only hard wheat flour (or a mixture of
hard and soft wheat, as in all-purpose flour) provides yeast
breads with enough protein to form a strong gluten
meshwork. Flour is available in many forms:

All-Purpose Flour. All-purpose flour, a mixture of hard and
soft wheat, can be used for all types of baking from light
cakes to hearty breads. As its name implies, it's designed to
be all purpose. It comes bleached as well as unbleached.

BLEACHED. Although this flour contains hard wheat, it is
not good for making yeast breads. The bleach shortens
the gluten strands keeping the bread from rising
properly.

UNBLEACHED. I use unbleached flour, with no bromates
or chemical additives, for most all of my baking needs.
It is versatile and dependable. I know I can expect
good results.

Bread Flour. Bread flour, made with hard wheat, works
well for yeast breads, but only if it is free of chemicals and
bromates. I get the same results from unbleached all-
purpose flour which is often less expensive.

Whole-Wheat Flour. Whole-wheat is available as a hard wheat and soft wheat flour. The hard whole-wheat flour is higher in protein than all-purpose flour, but the germ and bran will make a denser loaf. For a lighter loaf, I use a finely ground whole-wheat flour, or mix my whole-wheat flour with unbleached all-purpose flour.

Soft Wheat Flour. There are several varieties of soft wheat flour: cake flour, pastry flour, and self-rising flour. Each kind does a great job for its purpose, but does not work well in yeast breads.

Specialty Flours. There are many specialty flours that are flavorful and nutritious to work with in bread baking (rye, oat, millet, buckwheat, etc.). Wheat flour, however, is the only flour that forms the necessary gluten meshwork that is so important in bread baking. You can combine specialty flours with wheat flour. I recommend using 60% wheat flour to 40% specialty flour – the more specialty flour, the heavier the loaf.

LIQUIDS. Liquids stimulate the gluten formation, cause yeast to ferment, and affect other qualities of bread. For example, milk adds nutrition, aids in browning the crust, and extends the bread's keeping quality. Water provides an earthy flavor and makes the crust crispier. Potato water (water in which potatoes have been boiled) makes the loaf slightly larger and the texture more velvety. Recipes may call for other liquids, such as yogurt, buttermilk, sour cream, beer, fruit, and vegetable juices or purées.

SWEETENERS. Sweeteners activate the yeast, aid in browning the crust, and bring out the flavor of other ingredients. Granulated, brown, and raw sugars are interchangeable in equal measurements. Powdered sugar and confectioner's sugars are pulverized granulated sugar with a bit of cornstarch added to prevent it from clumping together. You can also substitute honey, molasses, malt barley, and syrups (corn, cane, and maple) for sugar, but since these sweeteners are liquid, your dough may require extra flour. Since liquid sweeteners are more concentrated, you can use less in your recipe.

SALT. Salt controls fermentation, slows down the rising time, and brings out the flavor of other ingredients. I use a scant teaspoon of salt for every 4 cups of flour in a recipe. If the recipe calls for more salt than that, you can safely reduce the amount without affecting the flavor.

FAT. Fat (butter, margarine, lard, shortening, and oil) improves bread's keeping quality, makes it tender and light, and makes slicing easier. It also lubricates the gluten meshwork of the dough which helps the dough rise better.

EGGS. Eggs add flavor, color and improve the structure of the dough. They also help make the texture delicate and the crust tender.

OTHER. Try using other ingredients sparingly. You can add softened grain berries or groats (cover with boiling water, cover, and let cool before using in bread), cracked wheat, sprouts (alfalfa, mung bean, sprouted grains), wheat germ, bran, barley, millet, rice (cooked, or ground and toasted), cornmeal, buckwheat, oats (whole grain, flour, rolled, steelcut), or soy (flour, meal). Each ingredient you add to a recipe will modify the behavior of the dough, as well as the texture, flavor, and appearance of the final product. It's best to experiment in small amounts!

*   *   *

Before we roll up our sleeves and start baking, there's one more area to cover: technique. Developing "good baking habits" is just as important as knowing your utensils and ingredients. The following tips and techniques are designed to help you better understand the process of preparing and baking bread - and to help you achieve certainty in the kitchen!

TIPS AND TECHNIQUES

RULES OF THUMB. There are four general rules of thumb to follow when baking yeast breads: activate the yeast, knead the dough properly, don't add too much flour, and make sure the bread is done before you take it out of the oven.

The first and last rules are simple to master if you have an instant-read thermometer. When activating yeast, make sure the liquid you add to it is 105 to 115 degrees. If you are using the quick-rise method (see *Yeast* under "Ingredients" on page 16), the other dry ingredients insulate the yeast, so your liquid should be between 120 and 130 degrees. To ensure that your bread is done, lift the loaf and push the instant-read thermometer up through the bottom of the bread to the center (don't worry, it won't leave a big hole). When the bread's internal temperature reaches 190 degrees, it's ready to come out of the oven.

KNEADING THE DOUGH. The second rule of thumb is essential to master. If the dough isn't kneaded well, the bread will not rise to its fullest potential and you'll have more crumbs on the cutting board than in the loaf itself. It takes a proficient kneader at least 8 to 10 minutes to knead the dough properly.

The process of kneading is important because of what happens as you do it. Kneading makes tiny blisters form throughout the dough that fill with gas formed by the yeast. The gas is what makes the dough rise. When you make a white bread, you can actually see the blisters just under the skin of the dough (they look like the small blisters that form on your arm when you get splattered by hot grease!).

After you have turned your dough out onto a well-floured work surface, begin kneading:

1. With your fingertips, pull the far edge of the dough toward you, folding it in half.
2. Using the heel of your hands, push the dough away from you with a rolling motion. This action should roll the dough over, not squish it down toward the work surface.
3. With your fingertips, flip the far edge of the dough over toward you.
4. Repeat steps 2 and 3 until the dough becomes long. Then, give the dough a quarter turn and, starting with step 1, continue repeating steps until dough becomes smooth and elastic.

It is important to develop a steady rhythm when kneading. Not only is it therapeutic, but it helps keep the dough from sticking to the work surface. Each person will develop his or her own rhythm: some people use a four count (fold-1, push-2, pull-3, turn-4), while others use an eight count. I prefer a light waltz! - fold-1, push-2, pull-3, push-4, pull-5, turn-6.

ADDING FLOUR. If the dough becomes sticky while you're kneading, sprinkle the work surface with a *very* light coating of flour. Once you have started the kneading process, you should add very little flour to your dough. Being able to "sense" how much flour your dough needs is the key to successful baking. Many bakers who rely solely on recipes fear the idea of making bread by feel. But, there is good reason to learn how: flour is finicky.

- different flours absorb liquids at various rates
- the age of the flour affects absorption
- weather affects how flour behaves in dough
- cookbook authors measure flour in a variety of ways

There are two ways to ensure that you don't add too much flour to your dough. The first way is to correctly measure flour when combining ingredients. Be careful not to pack flour into a dry measuring cup. Lightly spoon the flour into the cup, then swipe across the rim with a flat blade. If you scoop flour out of the bag with a 1-cup measuring cup, the flour will weigh about 5 ounces. By spooning flour into the same cup, it will weigh about 4 ounces. This makes a big difference if your recipe calls for six cups of flour - scooping will give you a cup or more too much.

The other way to make sure you aren't adding too much flour is to "test" your dough after kneading it for a while. Push the dough into a football shape and drop it on its end onto the work surface. Let it settle (if it doesn't settle, you've already added too much flour - oops!). If the top surface remains slightly rounded, you have added enough flour no matter how sticky the dough is. The dough should always be tacky to the touch before rising. You can also think of it this way: if you were making a free-standing loaf of bread (one without a pan), would it keep its shape if you put it on the pan now or would it flatten out? If it would keep its shape, you don't need more flour.

Besides the general rules of thumb listed above, there are other techniques you can use to ensure that your breads come out looking and tasting scrumptious, such as properly rising, shaping, and baking the dough.

RISING. I've read many clever ways to help your bread rise better. My favorite was a story about a little old lady who wrapped her dough and bowl in an Army blanket and placed it on top of a heating pad. Other folks have suggested putting the dough in an oven with a pot of boiling water, putting the dough in an oven with the light on, and placing it in the microwave at 30% power for 2 minutes before letting it sit. Some people buy expensive "rising" boxes.

None of this is necessary! All you need is a bowl (preferably ceramic), one tablespoon of oil, and a tightly woven towel. Pour the oil into the bowl and use the dough to smear it around a bit. Cover it with the towel and put the bowl in a draft-free place. In about an hour, your dough should have doubled in size. If your dough doubles in less than an hour, your rising place is too warm. I use a warmed ceramic bowl placed on my countertop. I heat it by placing warm (not hot) water in it for about 5 minutes before drying it and putting the oil and dough in. It retains the cozy temperature needed during the rising period.

There are two methods for testing to see if your dough has doubled in size. The *old-fashioned method* entails pressing two fingertips about a half inch into the dough. If the dents stay, the dough is doubled. The only problem with this method is that the dents will appear and stay if the dough has doubled too much.

The *measure method* is more practical and accurate. After you have kneaded your dough (before it begins to rise), measure it in a measuring cup. You may have to measure it in pieces, but try to get as accurate a total as you can. Then, with your dough still out of the bowl, fill the bowl with twice as much water as you have dough. The water line is your doubled-in-size line (some people mark it with fingernail polish or indelible ink).

SHAPING THE DOUGH. I do two things at this point that differ from many other bakers. I don't punch the dough down, and I turn it from the rising bowl to a lightly oiled work surface.

Punching the dough down makes the gluten in the dough become elastic again (it's difficult to roll the dough when it's like this). If you have trouble rolling the dough, cover it with a towel and let it rest on the work surface for 5 minutes then try again.

I use a lightly oiled work surface rather than a lightly floured surface because the dough doesn't accept flour evenly after it has risen. A lightly oiled surface allows the dough to slide easily when I roll it out or round it up. The oil will absorb into the dough and disappear.

Shape your dough per the recipe directions. Any kneaded dough can be shaped into loaves (pan or freestanding), buns, or rolls. Most of the recipes in this book suggest approximately 6-7 cups of flour, which produces about 3 pounds of dough – enough to make two 1½-pound loaves, three 1-pound loaves, 18 hamburger or hotdog buns, or 36 dinner rolls.

Once you have shaped the dough, cover it with a tightly woven towel and allow it to rise until it is **almost** doubled in size, about 45 minutes. If it rises too long before going into the oven, it will fall like a cake sometimes does. If it does rise too long, you can turn it out, reshape it and let it rise again.

Slashing the top of a freestanding loaf before baking allows the dough to rise under controlled circumstances. If you don't give the gases and moisture a place to escape, they make their own. This is why you see loaves sometimes that look like they have a "blow out" on the side.

BAKING THE DOUGH. Before you bake your bread, make sure the oven is fully preheated (takes about ten minutes). Your breads will not bake properly if the oven hasn't reached the correct temperature. I recommend placing the oven racks in a position that will allow whatever you are baking to rest in the center of the oven. The rack will be lower for loaves, higher for rolls. This rule goes for any baked good (cookies, cakes, etc.). There should be at least one inch of air space around all sides of your pans for the air to flow evenly. If you use a baking stone, preheat your stone in the oven for a minimum of 30 minutes before you bake with it.

Here's the place to review the fourth rule of thumb: making sure the bread has finished baking. Check the center of your bread with an instant-read thermometer. When it reads 190 degrees, your bread is ready to come out of the oven. When I bake for my family, I just stick the thermometer in through the top of the bread. But, this leaves a small but unsightly hole. If you are giving your loaf as a gift, you can lift the loaf out of the pan and stick the thermometer into the bottom (don't do it from the end or every slice will have a hole in it!). Don't worry about your yeast bread falling like a cake. Once the crust has risen and set (a process called the "oven spring"), the bread will hold its shape.

COOLING AND STORING. As soon as the bread is done, remove it from the pan and put it on a rack to cool. This prevents the bread from sweating, which makes the crust become soggy. Let bread completely cool before wrapping it. The average loaf of bread takes about 5 hours to cool all the way through. If you freeze it before it has cooled, the bread will steam up in the center and freeze like an ice cube.

Once the bread has cooled completely you can wrap it for storage. Some sourdough and heavy peasant-type breads can be stored for a short time in a breadbox without being wrapped (i.e. if you plan to eat them soon). If you live in the South, be careful - the humidity makes bread get moldy quickly.

Plastic bags are the best way to store bread. The crust becomes soft when it is wrapped, but for sandwich loaves that's okay. If you like your loaf to have crisp crust, you need to make it and eat it the same day. I store my breads in freezer-weight zip-style bags. The new jumbo bags will even hold a large Challah loaf. Be sure to squeeze excess air from around the bread. Too much air makes bread go stale and invites mold. To remove most of the air, put the bread in a zip-style bag, put a straw in one end of the zip top and close the bag to the straw. Suck the air out of the bag, quickly remove the straw and pinch the top of the bag closed to seal it.

To reheat bread that has been frozen, first thaw it, wrapped in foil with the shiny side facing out. Put the foil wrapped package in a preheated 350-degree oven for 10 minutes. Open the foil and cook 5 minutes longer. Using the foil with the shiny side out reflects the heat rays so the bread heats through to the middle without further browning.

Refrigeration causes bread to go stale quickly. It's better to slice it and freeze it. You can take it from the freezer a slice at a time whenever you want it. It only takes five to ten minutes to thaw – or you can pop it in the toaster immediately.

Bits & Pieces

If you have too much dough to go into an oven at one time, it is best to cover one pan and place it in the refrigerator to slow down the rising. Remove it from the refrigerator about five minutes before the first pan is finished. Then, bake it like you did the first dough. Another solution is to shape half the dough and put the remaining half back into the bowl for a second rise. Shape the second dough about 30 to 45 minutes after the first so that it will be ready to go into the oven when the first one comes out.

Loaves &
Baguettes

Basic White Learning Loaf

Makes 2 Loaves

This is the perfect loaf for mastering your bread baking skills because you see the formation of blisters when kneading. Be sure to read the "Tips and Techniques" section of this book on page 19 for a comprehensive discussion of the bread making process.

2 scant tablespoons or 2 (¼-ounce) packages active dry yeast
½ cup warm water (about 110 degrees)
2 cups warm milk or water (about 110 degrees)
2 tablespoons vegetable oil or shortening
2 tablespoons granulated sugar
2 teaspoons salt
6 to 7 cups unbleached flour

1. In a large bowl, stir yeast into ½ cup water to soften. Add milk or water, oil or shortening, sugar, salt, and 3 cups flour. Beat vigorously for two minutes.

2. Gradually stir in flour, ¼ cup at a time, until the dough begins to pull away from the side of the bowl.

3. Turn the dough out onto a floured work surface. Knead, adding flour a little at a time, until you have a smooth, elastic dough.

4. Put the dough into an oiled bowl. Turn to coat the entire ball of dough with oil. Cover with a tightly woven towel and let rise until doubled, about one hour.

5. Turn the dough out onto a lightly oiled work surface and divide in half. To shape a standard loaf, roll each half with a rolling pin into a 10 by 14-inch rectangle. This removes the excess gases and gives a more uniform texture to the finished loaves. Roll up the dough into a 10-inch cylinder, and pinch

the loose edge to the loaf. Fold the ends of the loaf like a package by bringing each side into the center of the end then bringing the bottom layer of dough to the top and pinching it. Repeat with the other end of the dough and place, pinched-side down, into well-greased loaf pans. Cover with a tightly woven towel and let rise until almost doubled, about 45 minutes.

6. About 10 minutes before baking, preheat the oven to 375 degrees.

7. Bake for 25 minutes, or until the internal temperature of the loaves reaches 190 degrees.

8. Immediately remove bread from pans and cool on a rack.

NOTE: DOUGH CAN BE DIVIDED INTO THIRDS AND BRAIDED; DIVIDED INTO 18 PIECES, SHAPED INTO BALLS, PLACED ON BAKING SHEETS THEN FLATTENED SLIGHTLY FOR BUNS; OR DIVIDED INTO 36 PIECES AND SHAPED INTO DINNER ROLLS. BRAIDS WILL BAKE AT 375 DEGREES FOR ABOUT 35 MINUTES; BUNS AND ROLLS BAKE AT 400 DEGREES FOR 15 TO 20 MINUTES.

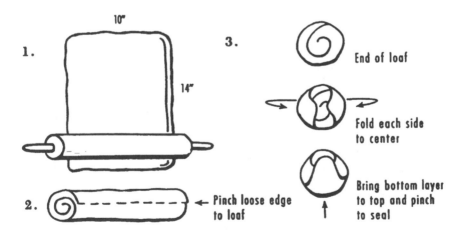

Carrot Ginger Bread

Ginger gives this bread a light, airy texture and carrots add a festive splash of color. These loaves make wonderful chicken salad sandwiches since the ginger and the chicken complement each other nicely.

2 scant tablespoons or 2 (¼-ounce) packages active dry yeast
½ cup warm water (about 110 degrees)
1½ cups warm milk (about 110 degrees)
2 tablespoons honey
2 tablespoons soft butter
2 teaspoons salt
2 cups peeled and finely shredded carrots
1 tablespoon ground ginger
5½ to 6½ cups unbleached flour

1. In a large bowl, stir yeast into water to soften. Add milk, honey, butter, salt, carrots, ginger and 3 cups flour. Beat vigorously for two minutes.

2. Gradually add flour ¼ cup at a time, until the dough begins to pull away from the side of the bowl.

3. Turn dough out onto a floured work surface and knead, adding flour as necessary, until you have a smooth, elastic dough.

4. Put dough into an oiled bowl. Turn to coat the entire ball of dough with oil. Cover with a tightly woven towel and let rise until doubled, about one hour.

5. Turn dough out onto a lightly oiled work surface and divide in half. Shape each half into a loaf and place into well-

greased loaf pans. Cover with a tightly woven towel and let rise until almost doubled, about 45 minutes.

6. About 10 minutes before baking, preheat oven to 375 degrees.

7. Bake for 25 minutes or until the internal temperature of the loaves reaches 190 degrees.

8. Immediately remove bread from pans and cool on a rack.

Bits & Pieces

"I'm forever amused and frustrated with the American term 'active' dry yeast. It wouldn't be much use if it were inactive!" *Elizabeth David, English Bread and Yeast Cookery*

Chonion Pepper Bread

For a quick snack or an elegant dinner party, this delicious jeweled bread does the trick. The coarse salt adds flavor and charm.

2 scant tablespoons or 2 (¼-ounce) packages active dry yeast
2½ cups warm water (about 110 degrees)
2 teaspoons salt
2 tablespoons honey
3 large eggs
2 cups whole wheat flour
4½ to 5½ cups unbleached flour
1½ cups seeded and coarsely chopped bell peppers*
1 cup coarsely chopped onion
4 cloves finely chopped garlic
2 cups ¼-inch cubes sharp cheddar cheese
Glaze - 1 egg beaten with 1 tablespoon cold water
Coarse salt (optional)

1. In a large bowl, stir yeast into water to soften. Add salt, honey, eggs, whole wheat flour and 1 cup unbleached flour. Beat vigorously for two minutes.

2. Add peppers, onion, garlic, and cheese. Stir until combined.

3. Gradually add flour, ¼ cup at a time, until the dough begins to pull away from the side of the bowl.

4. Turn dough out onto a floured work surface. Knead, adding flour a little at a time, until you have a smooth, elastic dough.

5. Put dough into an oiled bowl. Turn to coat the entire ball of dough with oil. Cover with a tightly woven towel and let rise until doubled, about one hour.

6. Turn dough out onto a lightly oiled work surface and divide in half. Shape each half into a round ball and place on a parchment-lined baking sheet. Flatten the top of the loaves slightly. Cover with a tightly woven towel and let rise until almost doubled, about 45 minutes.

7. About 10 minutes before baking, preheat oven to 375 degrees.

8. Just before baking, brush each loaf lightly with the glaze and sprinkle with coarse salt.

9. Bake for 25 minutes or until the internal temperature of the loaves reaches 190 degrees.

10. Immediately remove bread from baking sheets and cool on a rack.

*A mixture of colored peppers (red, green, orange, and yellow) makes this bread especially showy for entertaining.

County Fair Egg Bread

This is by far the loveliest bread I've made. It is named County Fair Egg Bread because this type of bread is often entered in fair bake-offs across the country. It usually wins too! The texture is stringy and velvety. The eggs produce a light golden yellow color.

2 scant tablespoons or 2 (¼-ounce) packages active dry yeast
½ cup warm water (about 110 degrees)
¼ cup granulated sugar
¼ cup soft butter
3 large eggs
1½ cups warm milk (about 110 degrees)
6½ to7½ cups unbleached flour
2 teaspoons salt
Glaze - one egg beaten with 1 tablespoon cold water
Poppy seeds or sesame seeds (optional)

1. In a large bowl, stir yeast into water to soften. Add sugar, butter, eggs, milk, and 3 cups flour (do not add the salt now). Beat vigorously for two minutes. This sponge has the consistency of a cake batter (see page 66 to learn more about sponges). Cover the sponge with plastic wrap and a tightly woven towel. Let rise for 25 minutes. It should be light and full of bubbles.

2. Add salt to the sponge and stir. The sponge will deflate. Gradually add flour, ¼ cup at a time, until the dough begins to pull away from the side of the bowl.

3. Turn the dough out onto a floured work surface. Knead, adding flour a little at a time, until you have a smooth, elastic dough.

4. Put dough into an oiled bowl. Turn to coat the entire ball of dough with oil. Cover with a tightly woven towel and let rise until doubled, about one hour.

5. Turn the dough out onto a lightly oiled work surface and divide into thirds. Shape each third into a strand 20 inches long. Lay the strands side-by-side on a well-greased baking sheet. Turn the baking sheet so the strands are facing lengthwise away from you. Starting in the center of the strands, place the right strand over the middle strand (note that the right strand has now become the middle strand), then the left strand over the middle, the right over the middle, left over the middle, etc. Continue this process until the strands are too short to braid. Pinch all three ends together and tuck them under.

6. To braid the other end of the loaf, turn the baking sheet around so that the unbraided portion is facing you. Place the middle strand over the right strand, then middle strand over the left, middle over the right, middle over the left, etc., until the ends are too short to braid. Pinch all three ends together and tuck them under. Cover with a tightly woven towel and let rise until almost doubled, about 45 minutes.

7. About 10 minutes before baking, preheat the oven to 375 degrees.

8. Just before baking, brush each loaf lightly with the egg glaze and sprinkle with seeds.

9. Bake for 45 minutes or until the internal temperature of the braid reaches 190 degrees.

10. Immediately remove braid from baking sheet and cool on a rack.

Garlic Baguettes

Makes 4 Thin Loaves

This bread is best served warm and fresh. Served cold, the garlic has a bitter taste. Reheat by placing the loaves directly on the rack in a 350-degree oven for 10 minutes. (If you don't have a baguette pan, use a baking sheet or two 8½ by 4½-inch loaf pans.)

2 scant tablespoons or 2 (¼-ounce) packages active dry yeast
2½ cups warm water (about 110 degrees)
2 teaspoons granulated sugar
4 teaspoons finely chopped garlic, *divided*
2 teaspoons salt
4 tablespoons olive oil, *divided*
6 to 7 cups unbleached flour

1. In a large bowl, stir yeast into water to soften. Add sugar, *2 teaspoons garlic*, salt, *2 tablespoons oil*, and 3 cups unbleached flour. Beat vigorously for two minutes.

2. Gradually add flour, ¼ cup at a time, until the dough begins to pull away from the side of the bowl.

3. Turn dough out onto a floured work surface. Knead, adding flour a little at a time, until you have a smooth, elastic dough.

4. Put dough into an oiled bowl. Turn to coat the entire ball of dough with oil. Cover with a tightly woven towel and let rise until doubled, about one hour.

5. Turn the dough out onto a lightly oiled work surface and divide in fourths. Shape each piece of dough into a 14-inch strand and place into well-greased baguette pans or

baking sheet. Cover with a tightly woven towel and let rise until almost doubled, about 45 minutes.

6. About 10 minutes before baking, preheat oven to 400 degrees. Place a shallow pan on the bottom shelf of the oven.

7. Just before baking, brush each loaf lightly with *olive oil.*

8. Place the bread in the oven and put 5 ice cubes into the pan on the bottom shelf. Close the door quickly to prevent steam from escaping.

9. Bake for 10 minutes.

10. Combine *remaining garlic* and *olive oil.* Remove the loaves from the oven and brush this mixture over entire surface of each loaf. Return the loaves to the oven and bake for 10 minutes, or until the internal temperature of the loaves reaches 190 degrees.

11. Immediately remove bread from pans and place on a rack. Brush with any remaining garlic-oil mixture. Allow the loaves to mellow 15 minutes before eating.

Bits & Pieces

Bread is low in calories. It's what you put on bread that's devastating. Certainly butter or margarine enhances bread, but unadorned bread or bread dipped in soup is wonderful, too.

Gruyere Baguettes

Gruyere cheese and rye have especially complementary flavors. But don't be in a rush to taste them! All cheese breads will have much more flavor if allowed to mellow for at least an hour after baking before you eat them.

2 scant tablespoons or 2 (¼-ounce) packages active dry yeast
2½ cups warm water (about 110 degrees)
¼ cup honey
2 tablespoons vegetable oil
2 teaspoons salt
2 cups rye flour
3½ to 4½ cups unbleached flour
2 cups shredded Gruyere cheese, *divided*
Cornmeal (optional)
Glaze ~ 1 egg beaten with 1 tablespoon olive oil

1. In a large bowl, stir yeast into water to soften. Add honey, oil, salt, rye flour, 2 cups unbleached flour, and *1 cup cheese*. Beat vigorously for two minutes.

2. Gradually add flour, ¼ cup at a time, until the dough begins to pull away from the side of the bowl.

3. Turn dough out onto a floured work surface. Knead, adding flour a little at a time, until you have a smooth, elastic dough.

4. Put dough into an oiled bowl. Turn to coat the entire ball of dough with oil. Cover with a tightly woven towel and let rise until doubled, about one hour.

5. Turn dough out onto a lightly oiled work surface and flatten to about ½-inch thick. Sprinkle with *remaining*

cheese and roll up into a cylinder. Knead the dough for two minutes to distribute the cheese (there should be streaks of cheese visible in the dough). Divide the dough in half, cover with a tightly woven towel, and let rest for 5 minutes.

6.   Grease baguette pans or a baking sheet. For a crunchier crust, sprinkle the pans lightly with cornmeal. Roll the dough with a rolling pin into an oval 2 inches shorter than the pan you are using. Roll up the oval into a long cylinder and pinch the seams to seal. Place loaves seam side down on prepared pans. Cover with a tightly woven towel and let rise until almost doubled, about 45 minutes.

7.   About 10 minutes before baking, preheat oven to 400 degrees.

8.   Just before baking, cut 3 or 4 diagonal slits, about ½-inch deep, into the top of each loaf. Brush each loaf lightly with the glaze.

9.   Bake for 20 minutes, or until the internal temperature of the loaves reaches 190 degrees.

10.   Immediately remove bread from pans and cool on a rack.

Herb Bread

Makes 2 Loaves

The tenderness of this bread goes well with many herbs. I particularly like the combination of sage, marjoram, and thyme, but you can substitute your favorites.

2 scant tablespoons or 2 (¼-ounce) packages active dry yeast
½ cup warm water (about 110 degrees)
2 cups warm milk (about 110 degrees)
½ cup vegetable shortening
2 tablespoons granulated sugar
2 teaspoons salt
6 to 7 cups unbleached flour
1 tablespoon fresh rubbed sage or 1 teaspoon rubbed dried sage
1 tablespoon fresh marjoram leaves or 1 teaspoon crushed dried marjoram leaves
1 tablespoon fresh thyme leaves or 1 teaspoon dried thyme leaves

1. In a large bowl, stir the yeast into water to soften. Add milk, shortening, sugar, salt, and 2 cups flour.

2. Whisk herbs with 1 cup flour until well blended. Add to yeast mixture and beat vigorously for two minutes.

3. Gradually add flour, ¼ cup at a time, until the dough begins to pull away from the side of the bowl.

4. Turn dough out onto a floured work surface. Knead, adding flour a little at a time, until you have a smooth, elastic dough.

5. Put dough into an oiled bowl. Turn to coat the entire ball of dough with oil. Cover with a tightly woven towel and let rise until doubled, about one hour.

6. Turn the dough out onto a lightly oiled work surface and divide in half. Shape each half into a loaf and place into

well-greased loaf pans. Cover with a tightly woven towel and let rise until almost doubled, about 45 minutes.

7. About 10 minutes before baking, preheat oven to 375 degrees.

8. Bake for 25 minutes, or until the internal temperature of the loaves reaches 190 degrees.

9. Immediately remove bread from pans and cool on a rack.

Bits & Pieces

Don't wash bread pans with soap unless absolutely necessary. Pans build up a natural patina and become dull (dirty looking!). Dull pans absorb heat and produce a dark crisp crust. If something needs to be scrubbed off the pans, use a mixture of equal parts of salt and oil. Rinse with hot water and dry immediately.

Honey Curry Bread

Makes 2 Loaves

My husband, Keith, and I love the deep, rich, spicy flavor of curry. This bread was developed using a few of the condiments that we use when having a meat curry. Whenever I mention tart apples, I usually use Granny Smith's because I like their sharp taste and firm texture.

2 scant tablespoons or 2 (¼-ounce) packages active dry yeast
½ cup warm water (about 110 degrees)
¼ cup soft butter
½ cup honey
2 cups warm buttermilk (about 110 degrees)
2 teaspoons salt
2 tablespoons curry powder
½ cup coarsely chopped onion
1 cup coarsely chopped tart apple
1 cup shredded coconut
1 cup raisins
1 cup slivered almonds
6½ to 7½ cups unbleached flour
Glaze - 1 egg beaten with 2 teaspoons water
Coarsely chopped almonds (optional)

1. In a large bowl, stir yeast into water to soften. Add butter, honey, buttermilk, salt, curry powder, onion, apple, coconut, raisins, almonds, and 3 cups flour. Beat vigorously for two minutes.

2. Gradually add flour, ¼ cup at a time, until the dough begins to pull away from the side of the bowl.

3. Turn dough out onto a floured work surface. Knead, adding flour a little at a time, until you have a smooth, elastic dough.

4. Put dough into an oiled bowl. Turn to coat the entire ball of dough with oil. Cover with a tightly woven towel and let rise until doubled, about one hour.

5. Turn the dough out onto a lightly oiled work surface and divide in half. Shape each half into a ball and place on a parchment-lined baking sheet. Flatten the top of the loaves slightly. Cover with a tightly woven towel and let rise until almost doubled, about 45 minutes.

6. About 10 minutes before baking, preheat oven to 375 degrees.

7. Just before baking, brush each loaf with the glaze and sprinkle with almonds. Cut 3 slits, about ½-inch deep and 2 inches apart, into the top of each loaf.

8. Bake for 25 minutes, or until the internal temperature of the loaves reaches 190 degrees.

9. Immediately remove bread from baking sheet and cool on a rack.

Italian Bread

Makes 2 Loaves

The longer kneading period gives this bread a finer texture than other breads. Also, Europeans give their breads a longer, cooler rising time to allow the flavors to develop to their fullest. This bread forms a magnificent crust when it is baked in a La Cloche – the closest a home bread baker can come to using a steam induced professional oven (see the instructions below).

2 scant tablespoons or 2 (¼-ounce) packages active dry yeast
2½ cups warm water (about 110 degrees)
2 teaspoons salt
5 ½ to 6 ½ cups unbleached flour
Cornmeal (optional)
Glaze - 1 egg white beaten with 1 tablespoon olive oil

1.   In a large bowl, stir yeast into water to soften. Add salt and 2 cups flour. Beat vigorously for two minutes.

2.   Gradually add flour, ¼ cup at a time, until the dough begins to pull away from the side of the bowl.

3.   Turn dough out onto a floured work surface. Knead, adding flour a little at a time, until you have a smooth, elastic dough.

4.   Put dough into an oiled bowl. Turn to coat the entire ball of dough with oil. Cover with a tightly woven towel and let rise until doubled, about one hour.

5.   Turn dough out onto work surface and knead for 5 minutes. Return to bowl and cover with plastic wrap and tightly woven towel and put into the refrigerator. Let dough rise for 3 hours.

6. Turn the dough out onto a lightly oiled work surface and divide in half. Roll each portion of dough into a strand 2 inches shorter than the pan you plan to use. Sprinkle a baguette pan or baking sheet with cornmeal and place strands onto pans. Cover with a tightly woven towel and let rise until almost doubled, about 1 to 1½ hours.

7. About 10 minutes before baking, preheat oven to 400 degrees. Place a shallow pan on the bottom shelf of the oven.

8. Just before baking, slit the top of each loaf diagonally in three places about ¼-inch deep. Brush each loaf lightly with the glaze.

9. Place the bread in the oven and put five ice cubes into the pan on the bottom shelf. Close the door quickly to prevent steam from escaping.

10. Bake for 20 minutes, or until the internal temperature of the loaves reaches 190 degrees.

11. Immediately remove bread from pans and cool on a rack.

La Cloche Instructions:

1. Prepare dough following steps 1 through 5 above (to the point where you shape it). Form the dough into a ball. Sprinkle cornmeal on a pizza peel or a piece of parchment paper that has been cut to fit in the bottom of the La Cloche. Place the dough on the cornmeal, cover with a tightly woven towel and let rise until almost doubled, about 45 minutes.

2. WHILE THE DOUGH IS RISING, fill the dome of the La Cloche with water and let it sit (because of the handle on top, it is best to set the dome on a bowl to keep it from tipping over).

3. About 25 minutes before baking, preheat the oven to 400 degrees and place the bottom of the La Cloche in the oven.

4. When the dough has risen, make 3 or 4 slits (½-inch deep) on the top of the dough. Brush the loaf lightly with the glaze. Gently slide the dough onto the bottom of the La Cloche that has been in the oven. Pour the water out of the lid and immediately put the lid on the base without drying it.

5. Bake for 40 minutes. Uncover and bake 5 to 10 minutes longer or until the internal temperature reaches 190 degrees.

6. Immediately remove bread from the La Cloche and cool on a rack. While the loaf is cooling, it will crackle.

Bits & Pieces

There are no preservatives in homemade bread. Fat in bread, improves its keeping qualities. Italian and French-style breads don't stay crispy and fresh very long since they have no fat in the recipe.

Semolina Olive Bread

Makes 2 Loaves

Many Italian breads are made using a sponge sometimes referred to as a "Biga." This additional step allows more time for flavor to develop. See page 66 for more information on sponges. Italian semolina flour is ground finer than American brands. If you have access to a mill, have the flour ground very fine, otherwise, regular semolina flour will work (the texture of the loaf will be more coarse, but it won't affect the taste). NOTE: IF YOU USE THE FOIL PACKETS OF YEAST, YOU'LL USE PART OF THE PACKAGE FOR THE SPONGE AND THE REST IN THE BREAD. ALSO NOTE THAT THE SPONGE TAKES 8 TO 12 HOURS TO RIPEN.

FOR THE SPONGE:

1 teaspoon active dry yeast
¼ cup warm water (about 110 degrees)
1 cup unbleached flour

1. *8 TO 24 HOURS BEFORE BAKING THE BREAD,* stir the yeast into water to soften. Gradually add flour, ¼ cup at a time, until the dough begins to pull away from the side of the bowl.

2. Turn the dough out onto a floured work surface. Knead, adding flour, a little at a time, until the dough has absorbed the 1 cup of flour, about 5 minutes.

3. Put the dough into a large glass or pottery bowl. Cover lightly with plastic wrap and a tightly woven towel. Let the dough sit at room temperature for 8 to 24 hours. It will rise, but after a few hours it settles.

FOR THE BREAD:

1½ cups warm water (about 110 degrees)
1½ teaspoons active dry yeast
1 cup cold water (about 60 degrees)
1½ teaspoons salt
1 tablespoon sugar
2 cups pitted and chopped Sicilian brine-cured olives
2 cups semolina flour
4 to 5 cups unbleached flour
Additional semolina flour

1.   *ABOUT 3 HOURS BEFORE BAKING,* add the warm water
     to the sponge in the bowl. Squeeze your fingers through
     the dough until it has dissolved into the water. Sprinkle the
     yeast over this mixture and let it sit for 5 minutes. Stir.

2.   Add cold water, salt, sugar, olives, semolina flour, and 1
     cup unbleached flour. Beat vigorously for two minutes.

3.   Gradually add flour, ¼ cup at a time, until the dough
     begins to pull away from the side of the bowl.

4.   Turn dough out onto a floured work surface. Knead,
     adding flour a little at a time, until you have a smooth,
     elastic dough.

5.   Put dough into an oiled bowl. Turn to coat the entire ball
     of dough with oil. Cover with a tightly woven towel and let
     rise until doubled, about two hours.

6.   Turn the dough out onto a lightly oiled work surface and
     divide in half. Shape each half into a ball. Roll each ball of
     dough in semolina flour to coat the entire surface of the
     loaf and place on a well-greased baking sheet. Flatten the
     top of the loaves slightly. Cover with a tightly woven towel
     and let rise for 45 minutes.

7.   About 10 minutes before baking, preheat oven to 375
     degrees. Place a shallow pan on the bottom shelf of the
     oven.

8. Just before baking, cut 3 slits about ¼ inch deep and one inch apart, on top of each loaf.

9. Place the bread in the oven and put 5 *ice* cubes into the pan on the bottom shelf. Close the door quickly to prevent steam from escaping.

10. Bake for 25 minutes, or until the internal temperature of the loaves reaches 190 degrees.

11. Immediately remove bread from baking sheet and cool on a rack.

Breadbakers Have warmer buns!

Bits & Pieces

Stale bread makes excellent croutons, breadcrumbs, bread puddings, or French toast.

Semolina Cheese Baguettes

Makes 4 Thin Loaves

These baguettes have a nutty flavor (due to the semolina flour) that complements the subtle taste of the Swiss cheese. As with most cheese breads, let the loaves mellow for an hour after baking to let the flavors develop. NOTE: TO PREPARE MASHED POTATOES, SEE *"BITS & PIECES"* ON PAGE 159.

2 scant tablespoons or 2 (¼-ounce) packages active dry yeast
2 cups warm water (about 110 degrees)
1 cup warm mashed potatoes
3 large eggs
¼ cup soft butter
2 tablespoons granulated sugar
2 teaspoons salt
2 cups shredded Swiss cheese, *divided*
5½ to 6½ cups semolina flour
Glaze - 1 egg beaten with 1 tablespoon cold water

1. In a large bowl, stir yeast into water to soften. Add potatoes, eggs, butter, sugar, salt, *1 cup cheese*, and 2 cups flour. Beat vigorously for two minutes.

2. Gradually add flour, ¼ cup at a time, until the dough begins to pull away from the side of the bowl.

3. Turn dough out onto a floured work surface. Knead, adding flour a little at a time, until you have a smooth, elastic dough.

4. Put dough into an oiled bowl. Turn to coat the entire ball of dough with oil. Cover with a tightly woven towel and let rise until doubled, about one hour.

5. Turn the dough out onto a lightly oiled work surface and knead in the *remaining cheese* – the cheese should

become marbled throughout the dough, not smooth. Divide the dough into fourths. Cover with a tightly woven towel and let rest for five minutes on the work surface.

6.   Shape each portion of dough into a 16-inch strand. Place on well-greased baguette pans or baking sheet. Cover with a tightly woven towel and let rise until almost doubled, about 45 minutes.

7.   About 10 minutes before baking, preheat oven to 400 degrees. Place a shallow pan on the bottom shelf of the oven.

8.   Slit the top of each loaf diagonally in three places about ¼-inch deep with a sharp blade, and brush lightly with the glaze.

9.   Place the bread in the oven and put 5 ice cubes into the pan on the bottom shelf. Close the door quickly to prevent steam from escaping.

10.   Bake for 20 minutes, or until the internal temperature of the loaves reaches 190 degrees.

11.   Immediately remove bread from pans and cool on a rack.

Rosemary Raisin Bread

Makes 2 Loaves

I find the aroma of rosemary especially powerful when combined with the sweetness of raisins. This bread makes outstanding sandwiches and toast; however, I think it makes the best French toast I've ever tasted.

2 scant tablespoons or 2 (¼-ounce) packages active dry yeast
½ cup warm water (about 110 degrees)
2 cups warm milk (about 110 degrees)
½ cup vegetable shortening
¼ cup honey
2 teaspoons salt
1 tablespoon orange rind
1 tablespoon fresh chopped rosemary or 1 teaspoon dried
   rosemary
1½ cups golden sultana raisins
6-7 cups unbleached flour
Butter (optional)

1. In a large bowl, stir yeast into water to soften. Add milk, shortening, honey, salt, orange rind, rosemary, raisins, and 2 cups flour. Beat vigorously for two minutes.

2. Gradually add flour, ¼ cup at a time, until the dough begins to pull away from the side of the bowl.

3. Turn dough out onto a floured work surface. Knead, adding flour a little at a time, until you have a smooth, elastic dough.

4. Put dough into an oiled bowl. Turn to coat the entire ball of dough with oil. Cover with a tightly woven towel and let rise until doubled, about one hour.

5. Turn the dough out onto a lightly oiled work surface and divide in half. Shape each half into a loaf and place into well-

greased loaf pans. Cover with a tightly woven towel and let rise until almost doubled, about 45 minutes.

6. About 10 minutes before baking, preheat oven to 375 degrees.

7. Bake for 25 minutes, or until the internal temperature of the loaf reaches 190 degrees.

8. Immediately remove bread from pans and cool on a rack. For a soft shiny crust, rub the tops of the warm loaves with butter.

Bits & Pieces

Bread is extremely personal. Three people can follow the same recipe and end up with three entirely different masterpieces. The way each person measures (or doesn't measure), the method of mixing ingredients, the length of time bread is kneaded, the method of kneading, the types of pans, the weather, the oven, etc., affects the final product. Each bread is uniquely yours and no one else can make it the way you do!

Parmesan Potato Bread

Makes 2 Loaves

It's hard to stop nibbling this exquisite bread. The crust is crisp and the bits of potato are slightly crunchy. I love to eat the crust first, then start dipping the soft, sweet insides into a favorite soup...it's heaven! For a slightly marbled texture, use shredded Parmesan rather than finely grated.

2 scant tablespoons or 2 (¼-ounce) packages active dry yeast
2 cups warm water (about 110 degrees)
2 teaspoons salt
1 tablespoon finely minced garlic
1 tablespoon finely chopped fresh rosemary or 1 teaspoon dried
  rosemary
¼ cup olive oil
2 cups coarsely shredded raw potato
1 cup finely shredded or grated Parmesan cheese
6 to 7 cups unbleached flour
Additional olive oil

1.   In a large bowl, stir yeast into water to soften. Add salt, garlic, rosemary, olive oil, potato, cheese, and 3 cups flour. Beat vigorously for two minutes.

2.   Gradually add flour, ¼ cup at a time, until the dough begins to pull away from the side of the bowl.

3.   Turn dough out onto a floured work surface. Knead, adding flour a little at a time, until you have a smooth, elastic dough.

4.   Put dough into an oiled bowl. Turn to coat the entire ball of dough with oil. Cover with a tightly woven towel and let rise until doubled, about one hour.

5.   Turn the dough out onto a lightly oiled work surface and divide in half. Shape each half into a ball and place onto a well-greased baking sheet. Cover with a tightly woven towel and let rise until almost doubled, about 45 minutes.

6.   About 10 minutes before baking, preheat oven to 375 degrees. Place a shallow pan on the bottom shelf of the oven.

7.   Just before baking, brush each loaf liberally with extra olive oil and cut a cross about ¼-inch deep into the top.

8.   Place the bread in the oven and put 5 ice cubes into the pan on the bottom shelf. Close the door quickly to prevent steam from escaping.

9.   Bake for 25 minutes, or until the internal temperature of the loaves reaches 190 degrees.

10.   Immediately remove bread from baking sheet and cool on a rack.

Sundried Tomato and Caramelized Onion Bread

Makes 2 Loaves

The tart tomatoes and sweet onions combine to make this bread a gutsy full-bodied loaf that goes well with meats and cheeses. If you're using sundried tomatoes packed in oil, use the oil to sauté the onions rather than the olive oil called for in the recipe.

2 cups thinly sliced onion rings
½ cup sundried tomatoes
2 tablespoons olive oil
1 tablespoon brown sugar
2 scant tablespoons or 2 (¼-ounce) packages active dry yeast
½ cup warm water (about 110 degrees)
2 cups warm milk (about 110 degrees)
2 teaspoons salt
2 tablespoons granulated sugar
6 to 7 cups unbleached flour
Additional olive oil (optional)

1. In a skillet over medium-low heat, sauté the onions and sundried tomatoes in oil for three minutes. Sprinkle with brown sugar and continue to cook until the onions are transparent and golden in color, about 5 more minutes. Set aside to cool.

2. In a large bowl, stir yeast into water to soften. Add onion mixture, milk, salt, granulated sugar, and 3 cups flour. Beat vigorously for two minutes.

3. Gradually add flour, ¼ cup at a time, until the dough begins to pull away from the side of the bowl.

4. Turn dough out onto a floured work surface. Knead, adding flour a little at a time, until you have a smooth, elastic dough.

5. Put dough into an oiled bowl. Turn to coat the entire ball of dough with oil. Cover with a tightly woven towel and let rise until doubled, about one hour.

6. Turn the dough out onto a lightly oiled work surface and divide in half. Shape each half into a ball and place on a well-greased baking sheet. Flatten the top of the loaves slightly. Cover with a tightly woven towel and let rise until almost doubled, about 45 minutes.

7. About 10 minutes before baking, preheat oven to 375 degrees.

8. Just before baking, brush the tops of each loaf lightly with olive oil. Cut ¼-inch deep slits in a grid pattern (see picture below) into the top of each loaf.

9. Bake for 25 minutes, or until the internal temperature of the loaf reaches 190 degrees.

10. Immediately remove bread from pans and cool on a rack.

Pull-Apart Bread

Makes 1 Large Loaf

This bread is versatile (it can be served with almost any dish) and is fun to eat because you get to pull it apart! This bread is a basic white bread. You can substitute your favorite whole wheat recipe as long as you follow step 5. You have a choice between a sweet and a savory variation (see below).

2 scant tablespoons or 2 (¼-ounce) packages active dry yeast
½ cup warm water (about 110 degrees)
1½ cups warm milk (about 110 degrees)
2 tablespoons vegetable shortening
2 tablespoons granulated sugar
2 teaspoons salt
4½ to 5½ cups unbleached flour
½ cup melted butter
Either the Savory or Sweet Coating (listed below)

Savory Coating: 1 cup finely grated Parmesan cheese tossed with ½ cup finely chopped fresh parsley and 1 teaspoon finely chopped garlic

OR

Sweet Coating: 1 cup granulated sugar mixed with 2 tablespoons cinnamon

1. In a large bowl, stir yeast into water to soften. Add milk, shortening, sugar, salt, and 2 cups flour. Beat vigorously for two minutes.

2. Gradually add flour, ¼ cup at a time, until the dough begins to pull away from the side of the bowl.

3. Turn dough out onto a floured work surface. Knead, adding flour a little at a time, until you have a smooth, elastic dough.

4. Put dough into an oiled bowl. Turn to coat the entire ball of dough with oil. Cover with a tightly woven towel and let rise until doubled, about one hour.

5. Turn the dough out onto a lightly oiled work surface and divide into 72 equal pieces. Shape each piece into a ball. Dip the balls in melted butter, then roll in either the Savory or Sweet mixture (whichever you choose). Stack the balls in a well-greased bundt or tube pan. Cover with a tightly woven towel and let rise until almost doubled, about 45 minutes.

6. About 10 minutes before baking, preheat oven to 375 degrees.

7. Bake for 35 minutes, or until the internal temperature of the loaves reaches 190 degrees.

8. Allow to cool in the pan for 5 minutes. Remove the loaf from pan and place the loaf bottom-side-up on a rack to cool. Let the loaf mellow for 15 minutes before serving. To eat, put the bread on a plate and let each person pull the balls off.

Happiness Is
Being Kneaded!

Sesame Cheddar Bread

Makes 2 Loaves

Without a doubt, this is one of my family's favorite breads. They love the flavor of toasted sesame seeds and sharp Cheddar cheese. The cheese is added in two stages producing a mild cheese-flavored dough with large shreds of cheese marbled throughout.

2 scant tablespoons or 2 (¼-ounce) packages active dry yeast
2 cups warm water (about 110 degrees)
¼ cup granulated sugar
2 tablespoons soft butter
2 teaspoons salt
2 eggs, slightly beaten
½ cup sesame seeds, toasted (see "Bits & Pieces" on next page)
5½ to 6½ cups unbleached flour
3 cups shredded Cheddar cheese, *divided*

1. In a large bowl, stir yeast into water to soften. Add sugar, butter, salt, eggs, sesame seeds, 2 cups flour and *2 cups cheese*. Beat vigorously for two minutes.

2. Gradually add flour, ¼ cup at a time, until the dough begins to pull away from the side of the bowl.

3. Turn dough out onto a floured work surface. Knead, adding flour a little at a time, until you have a smooth, elastic dough.

4. Put dough into an oiled bowl. Turn to coat the entire ball of dough with oil. Cover with a tightly woven towel and let rise until doubled, about one hour.

5. Turn the dough out onto a lightly oiled work surface. With the heel of your hand, flatten the dough to a 15-inch square. Sprinkle with the *remaining cheese*. Roll up, then knead a

few times to marble the cheese throughout the dough. Cover with a tightly woven towel and let rest for 5 minutes.

6. Divide dough in half. Shape each half into a loaf and place into well-greased loaf pans. Cover with a tightly woven towel and let rise until almost doubled, about 45 minutes.

7. About 10 minutes before baking, preheat oven to 375 degrees.

8. Bake for 25 minutes, or until the internal temperature of the loaves reaches 190 degrees.

9. Immediately remove bread from pans and cool on a rack.

Bits & Pieces

To toast sesame seeds, put them in a small saucepan over medium heat. Stir occasionally until the seeds turn a golden color, about 7 minutes. Cool before using in yeast dough. Heat kills the yeast.

Buttermilk Orange Wheat Bread

Makes 2 loaves

The sweet taste of orange rind in this hearty recipe complements the subtle tartness of the buttermilk and the nutty taste of the whole wheat. **NOTE:** WHEN HEATED, BUTTERMILK OFTEN SEPARATES OR LOOKS CURDLED. THAT'S OKAY, USE IT ANYWAY, WON'T AFFECT THE FINAL PRODUCT!

2 scant tablespoons or 2 (¼-ounce) packages active dry yeast
1 cup warm water (about 110 degrees)
2 cups warm buttermilk (about 110 degrees)
¼ cup honey
3 tablespoons vegetable oil
2 teaspoons salt
1 tablespoon grated orange peel
½ cup finely cracked wheat
2 cups whole wheat flour
4 to 5 cups unbleached flour
Glaze - 1 egg white beaten with 1 teaspoon cold water
Cracked wheat (optional)

1. In a large bowl, stir yeast into water to soften. Add buttermilk, honey, oil, salt, orange peel, cracked wheat, whole wheat flour, and 1 cup unbleached flour. Beat vigorously for two minutes.

2. Gradually add flour, ¼ cup at a time, until the dough begins to pull away from the side of the bowl.

3. Turn dough out onto a floured work surface. Knead, adding flour a little at a time, until you have a smooth, elastic dough.

4. Put dough into an oiled bowl. Turn to coat the entire ball of dough with oil. Cover with a tightly woven towel and let rise until doubled, about one hour.

5. Punch the dough down and knead it briefly on a lightly oiled surface. Return it to the bowl, cover with a tightly woven towel and let rise for 25 minutes. (The second rise helps develop flavor and produces a finer textured loaf. It also gives the cracked wheat more time to soften.)

6. Turn the dough out onto a lightly oiled work surface and divide in half. Shape each half into a loaf and place into well-greased loaf pans. Cover with a tightly woven towel and let rise until almost doubled, about 45 minutes.

7. About 10 minutes before baking, preheat the oven to 375 degrees.

8. Just before baking, brush each loaf lightly with the egg glaze and sprinkle with cracked wheat.

9. Bake for 25 minutes or until the internal temperature of the loaves reaches 190 degrees.

10. Immediately remove from pans and cool on a rack.

Bits & Pieces

Rough-skinned, porous lemons and oranges have a thicker rind that is easier to cut off or grate; however, they also have less juice than smoother ones.

Coconut Sunflower Seed Wheat Loaf

Makes 2 Loaves

This robust sandwich loaf offers a slightly sweet flavor that complements roasted meats such as roast beef or turkey. However, I feel it really is at its best when toasted and slathered with butter. This is a hearty bread so take care not to add too much flour or you will end up with a heavy loaf.

2 cups scalded milk*
½ cup honey
½ cup cracked wheat
2 scant tablespoons or 2 (¼-ounce) packages active dry yeast
½ cup warm water (about 110 degrees)
¾ cup shredded coconut
2 teaspoons salt
¾ cup toasted wheat germ
½ cup toasted sunflower seeds
5 to 6 cups unbleached flour
Glaze - 1 large egg beaten with 1 tablespoon cold water
Additional wheat germ (optional)

1.   Combine milk, honey, and cracked wheat. Cover and cool to 110 degrees.

2.   In a large bowl, stir yeast into water to soften. Add milk mixture, coconut, salt, wheat germ, sunflower seeds, and 2 cups flour. Beat vigorously for two minutes.

3.   Gradually add flour, ¼ cup at a time, until the dough begins to pull away from the side of the bowl.

4.   Turn dough out onto a floured work surface. Knead, adding flour a little at a time, until you have a smooth, elastic dough.

5.   Put dough into an oiled bowl. Turn to coat the entire ball of dough with oil. Cover with a tightly woven towel and let rise until doubled, about one hour.

6.   Turn the dough out onto a lightly oiled work surface and divide in half. Shape each half into a loaf and place into well-greased loaf pans. Cover with a tightly woven towel and let rise until almost doubled, about 45 minutes.

7.   About 10 minutes before baking, preheat oven to 375 degrees.

8.   Just before baking, brush the tops of each loaf lightly with the glaze and sprinkle with wheat germ.

9.   Bake for 25 minutes, or until the internal temperature of the loaves reaches 190 degrees.

10. Immediately remove bread from pans and cool on a rack.

*To scald milk, heat until just before it comes to a boil, and remove from heat.

Bits & Pieces

Plastic bags make crusts soft, which is fine for sandwich loaves that usually have a soft crust anyhow.

Cracked Wheat Bread

Makes 2 Loaves

This bread is made with a sponge, which gives its marvelous tangy flavor plenty of time to develop. A sponge is a batterlike mixture made by combining yeast and some of the recipe's ingredients. Usually salt is omitted from a sponge to allow the mixture to rise quickly. Sponges may rise anywhere from 30 minutes up to 8 hours. During this time the sponge becomes frothy and full of bubbles. When the sponge is allowed to rise for over 2 hours, the mixture will usually fall or deflate. Don't be concerned. The sponge will reactivate when the remaining ingredients are added later. NOTE: THE SPONGE TAKES 8 TO 24 HOURS TO RIPEN.

FOR THE SPONGE:

1 scant tablespoon or 1 (¼-ounce) package active dry yeast
2 cups warm water (about 110 degrees)
¾ cup cracked wheat
2 cups unbleached flour

1. Combine yeast, water, cracked wheat, and flour in a large bowl, and beat vigorously for two minutes. Cover tightly with plastic wrap and let rise from 8 to 24 hours at room temperature. This sponge has the consistency of a cake batter.

FOR THE BREAD:

1 scant tablespoon or 1 (¼-ounce) package active dry yeast
½ cup warm water (about 110 degrees)
2 tablespoons honey
2 tablespoons vegetable oil
2 teaspoons salt
1 cup whole wheat flour
1½ to 2½ cups unbleached flour

1. In a large bowl, stir yeast into water to soften. Add starter, honey, oil, salt, and whole wheat flour. Beat vigorously for two minutes.

2. Gradually add unbleached flour, ¼ cup at a time, until the dough begins to pull away from the side of the bowl.

3. Turn dough out onto a floured work surface. Knead, adding flour a little at a time, until you have a smooth, elastic dough.

4. Put dough into an oiled bowl. Turn to coat the entire ball of dough with oil. Cover with a tightly woven towel and let rise until doubled, about one hour.

5. Turn the dough out onto a lightly oiled work surface and divide in half. Shape each half into a loaf and place into well-greased loaf pans. Cover with a tightly woven towel and let rise until almost doubled, about 45 minutes.

6. About 10 minutes before baking, preheat oven to 375 degrees.

7. Bake for 25 minutes, or until the internal temperature of the loaves reaches 190 degrees.

8. Immediately remove bread from pans and cool on a rack.

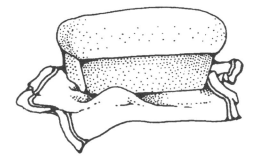

Maple Wheat Berry Bread

Makes 2 Loaves

Wheat berries are available in health food stores or by mail order (see "Sources" on page 182). Softened wheat berries add nutrients and a hearty texture to the bread.

1 cup wheat berries
3 cups boiling water
2 scant tablespoons or 2 (¼-ounce) packages active dry yeast
2½ cups warm water (about 110 degrees)
½ cup pure maple syrup
¼ cup vegetable oil
2 teaspoons salt
5½ to 6½ cups unbleached flour

1. Cover wheat berries with boiling water and allow to sit for three hours. The berries will almost double in size. Drain them completely. Place on a towel to remove moisture. (This can be done up to 5 days prior to baking. Store in an airtight container or bag in the refrigerator.)

2. When ready to make the bread, combine the softened wheat berries with 1 cup flour. If you have a food processor, you can process all of the mixture using the metal blade for 1 to two minutes depending on how much texture you like in your bread. If using a blender, you must process in smaller batches (divide the berry/flour mixture into fourths, blend for one to two minutes, depending on how much texture you want. You can also use a sharp knife to chop wheat berries, but the process is messy since the berries have a mind of their own and want to scurry away!

3. In a large bowl, stir yeast into water to soften. Add the syrup, oil, salt, chopped wheat berries, and 2 cups flour. Beat vigorously for two minutes.

4. Gradually add flour, ¼ cup at a time, until the dough begins to pull away from the side of the bowl.

5. Turn dough out onto a floured work surface. Knead, adding flour a little at a time, until you have a smooth, elastic dough.

6. Put dough into an oiled bowl. Turn to coat the entire ball of dough with oil. Cover with a tightly woven towel and let rise until doubled, about one hour.

7. Turn the dough out onto a lightly oiled work surface and divide in half. Shape each half into a loaf and place into well-greased loaf pans. Cover with a tightly woven towel and let rise until almost doubled, about 45 minutes.

8. About 10 minutes before baking, preheat oven to 375 degrees.

9. Bake for 25 minutes, or until the internal temperature of the loaves reaches 190 degrees.

10. Immediately remove bread from pans and cool on a rack.

Chewy Oatmeal Bread

Makes 2 Loaves

Uncooked oats not only add extra vitamins, minerals, and fiber when added to breads, they also add a wonderful chewy texture. Oats also contain a natural antioxidant that extends the shelf-life of the bread.

2 scant tablespoons or 2 (¼-ounce) packages active dry yeast
2½ cups warm water (about 110 degrees)
¼ cup vegetable shortening
¼ cup brown sugar
2 teaspoons salt
1 cup thick rolled oats
1 cup whole wheat flour
4½ to 5½ cups unbleached flour
Additional rolled oats (optional)

1. In a large bowl, stir yeast into water to soften. Add shortening, sugar, salt, oats, whole wheat flour and 2 cups unbleached flour. Beat vigorously for two minutes.

2. Gradually add flour, ¼ cup at a time, until the dough begins to pull away from the side of the bowl.

3. Turn dough out onto a floured work surface. Knead, adding flour a little at a time, until you have a smooth, elastic dough.

4. Put dough into an oiled bowl. Turn to coat the entire ball of dough with oil. Cover with a tightly woven towel and let rise until doubled, about one hour.

5. Turn the dough out onto a lightly oiled work surface and divide in half. Shape each half into a ball. Briefly hold each ball of dough under cold running water then roll in additional rolled oats. Place on well-greased baking sheets (do not flatten the tops of these loaves). Cover with a tightly

woven towel and let rise until almost doubled, about 45 minutes.

6. About 10 minutes before baking, preheat oven to 375 degrees.

7. Just before baking cut a cross about ½-inch deep across each loaf.

8. Bake for 25 minutes, or until the internal temperature of the loaf reaches 190 degrees.

9. Immediately remove bread from baking sheet and cool on a rack.

Bits & Pieces

Dr. Samuel Johnson, author of *Dictionary of English Language* once commented to the Lord Mayor of Edinburgh, James Boswell: "Oatmeal! Food for horses in England and men in Scotland." Whereupon the Scot replied: "Aye, and where do you find such horses or such men?"

Whole Wheat Raisin Nut Bread

Makes 2 Loaves

This bread is somewhat sweet and quite moist making it ideal for toast. I use this bread for egg salad sandwiches with lettuce. When I was a child, my mother used to take me to Rich's Magnolia Room in downtown Atlanta where I'd order an egg salad sandwich on whole wheat raisin bread. It brings back many happy memories!

2 scant tablespoons or 2 (¼-ounce) packages active dry yeast
2½ cups warm water (about 110 degrees)
½ cup brown sugar, firmly packed
2 teaspoons salt
¼ cup vegetable shortening
2 cups whole wheat flour
4 to 5 cups unbleached flour
1½ cups raisins
1 cup coarsely chopped walnuts

1. In a large bowl, stir yeast into water to soften. Add brown sugar, salt, shortening, whole wheat flour, and 1 cup unbleached flour. Beat vigorously for two minutes. Add the raisins and nuts and mix thoroughly.

2. Gradually add flour, ¼ cup at a time, until the dough begins to pull away from the side of the bowl.

3. Turn dough out onto a floured work surface. Knead, adding flour a little at a time, until you have a smooth, elastic dough.

4. Put dough into an oiled bowl. Turn to coat the entire ball of dough with oil. Cover with a tightly woven towel and let rise until doubled, about one hour.

5. Turn the dough out onto a lightly oiled work surface and divide in half. Shape each half into a loaf and place into well-

greased loaf pans. Cover with a tightly woven towel and let rise until almost doubled, about 45 minutes.

6. About 10 minutes before baking, preheat oven to 375 degrees.

7. Bake for 25 minutes, or until the internal temperature of the loaves reaches 190 degrees.

8. Immediately remove bread from pans and cool on a rack.

Whole Wheat Seed Bread

Makes 2 Loaves

*This bread has a smooth, even texture and a deep, robust taste –
it's great toasted. Roasting and toasting seeds brings out their
flavor (see "Bits & Pieces" on next page for directions).*

2 scant tablespoons or 2 (¼-ounce) packages active dry yeast
2½ cups warm water (about 110 degrees)
2 large eggs
¼ cup vegetable oil
½ cup molasses
½ cup roasted sunflower seeds
½ cup toasted sesame seeds
¼ cup poppy seeds
2 teaspoons salt
2 cups whole wheat flour
3½ to 4½ cups unbleached flour

1. In a large bowl, stir yeast into water to soften. Add eggs, oil,
   molasses, sunflower seeds, sesame seeds, poppy seeds, salt,
   whole wheat flour and 1 cup unbleached flour. Beat
   vigorously for two minutes.

2. Gradually add flour, ¼ cup at a time, until the dough begins
   to pull away from the side of the bowl.

3. Turn dough out onto a floured work surface. Knead, adding
   flour a little at a time, until you have a smooth, elastic dough.

4. Put dough into an oiled bowl. Turn to coat the entire ball of
   dough with oil. Cover with a tightly woven towel and let rise
   until doubled, about one hour.

5. Turn the dough out onto a lightly oiled work surface and
   divide in half. Shape each half into a loaf and place into well-

greased loaf pans. Cover with a tightly woven towel and let rise until almost doubled, about 45 minutes.

6. About 10 minutes before baking, preheat oven to 375 degrees.

7. Bake for 25 minutes, or until the internal temperature of the loaves reaches 190 degrees.

8. Immediately remove bread from pans and cool on a rack.

Bits & Pieces

To roast sunflower seeds, spread them on a baking sheet and put them into a preheated 375-degree oven for 8 to 10 minutes. Watch towards the end of the time to make sure they don't over cook. Cool before using in bread.

To toast sesame seeds, put them in a small saucepan over medium heat. Stir occasionally until the seeds turn a golden color, about 7 minutes. Cool before using in your dough. Heat kills the yeast.

10-Grain Orange Bread

Makes 2 Loaves

This grain recipe produces a robust, hearty loaf perfect for sandwiches and toast. The orange rind adds a pleasant fruity, fresh flavor.

2½ cups water, *divided*
2 cups 10-grain mix (see directions on next page)
2 scant tablespoons or 2 (¼-ounce) packages active dry yeast
2 teaspoons salt
¼ cup vegetable oil
2 large eggs
1 tablespoon grated orange rind
½ cup honey or brown sugar, firmly packed
4½ to 5½ cups unbleached flour

1. Bring *2 cups water* to a boil. Add grain mix, cover and cool to 110 degrees.

2. Heat remaining *½ cup water* to 110 degrees and combine with yeast in a large bowl to soften. Add cooled grain mix, salt, oil, eggs, orange rind, honey or brown sugar and 2 cups flour. Beat vigorously for two minutes.

3. Gradually add flour, ¼ cup at a time, until the dough begins to pull away from the side of the bowl.

4. Turn dough out onto a floured work surface. Knead, adding flour a little at a time, until you have a smooth, elastic dough.

5. Put dough into an oiled bowl. Turn to coat the entire ball of dough with oil. Cover with a tightly woven towel and let rise until doubled, about one hour.

6. Turn dough out onto a lightly oiled work surface and divide in half. Shape each half into a loaf and place into well-

greased loaf pans. Cover with a tightly woven towel and let rise until almost doubled, about 45 minutes.

7. About 10 minutes before baking, preheat oven to 375 degrees.

8. Bake for 25 minutes or until the internal temperature of the loaves reaches 190 degrees.

9. Immediately remove bread from pans and cool on a rack.

Betsy's 10-grain Mix

Makes Enough for 5 Recipes

You can mix your own mix or purchase a pre-made mixture in a health food store. Flakes are rolled grains and can be found in health-food stores or check the "Sources" on page 183. You can store this Mix in an airtight container for up to 6 months.

1 cup wheat flakes
1 cup triticale flakes
1 cup rye flakes
1 cup barley flakes
1 cup oatmeal
1 cup millet
1 cup stone-ground cornmeal
1 cup semolina flour
1 cup cracked wheat
1 cup soy flour

1. Combine all the ingredients and whisk to mix.

2. Place in an airtight container until ready to use.

Anadama Bread

There are many versions of how this bread got its name. They're all similar, but each varies slightly. The story goes that a woman from New England, named Anna, somehow provoked her husband - some say through laziness; others say that she baked the same bread daily, or she wouldn't finish baking her bread. The husband, in his anger, either threw a bag of cornmeal at her and missed, causing the cornmeal to fall into the dough, or he grabbed cornmeal instead of flour and tried to finish making the bread himself muttering "Anna, damn her!" The story origin may be uncertain, but the recipe of flour, cornmeal, yeast, and molasses has prevailed!

2 cups boiling water
½ cup dark molasses
2 teaspoons salt
¼ cup vegetable shortening
1 cup cornmeal
2 scant tablespoons or 2 (¼-ounce) packages active dry yeast
½ cup warm water (about 110 degrees)
5 to 6 cups unbleached flour

1. Combine boiling water, molasses, salt, shortening, and cornmeal. Stir to mix. Cover and cool to 110 degrees (about 45 minutes).

2. In a large bowl, stir yeast into water to soften. Add molasses mixture and 2 cups flour. Beat vigorously for two minutes.

3. Gradually add flour, ¼ cup at a time, until the dough begins to pull away from the side of the bowl.

4. Turn dough out onto a floured work surface. Knead, adding flour a little at a time, until you have a smooth, elastic dough.

5. Put dough into an oiled bowl. Turn to coat the entire ball of dough with oil. Cover with a tightly woven towel and let rise until doubled, about one hour.

6. Turn the dough out onto a lightly oiled work surface and divide in half. Shape each half into a loaf and place into well-greased loaf pans. Cover with a tightly woven towel and let rise until almost doubled, about 45 minutes.

7. About 10 minutes before baking, preheat oven to 375 degrees.

8. Bake for 25 minutes, or until the internal temperature of the loaves reaches 190 degrees.

9. Immediately remove bread from pans and cool on a rack.

Bits & Pieces

Lopsided loaves are OK - it happens to the best of us!

Banana Bran Bread

This bread combines the smooth taste of banana with the hearty texture of bran to create a nourishing sandwich bread. Shape into rolls for a breakfast or brunch treat.

2 scant tablespoons or 2 (¼-ounce) packages active dry yeast
½ cup warm water (about 110 degrees)
1 cup warm milk (about 110 degrees)
2 cups mashed ripe bananas
¼ cup soft butter
2 teaspoons salt
¼ cup granulated sugar
1 cup raw unprocessed bran
5½ to 6½ cups unbleached flour

1. In a large bowl, stir yeast into water to soften. Add milk, bananas, butter, salt, sugar, bran and 2 cups flour. Beat vigorously for two minutes.

2. Gradually add flour, ¼ cup at a time, until the dough begins to pull away from the side of the bowl.

3. Turn dough out onto a floured work surface. Knead, adding flour a little at a time, until you have a smooth, elastic dough.

4. Put dough into an oiled bowl. Turn to coat the entire ball of dough with oil. Cover with a tightly woven towel and let rise until doubled, about one hour.

5. Turn dough out onto a lightly oiled work surface and divide in half. Shape each half into a loaf and place into well-greased loaf pans. Cover with a tightly woven towel and let rise until almost doubled, about 45 minutes.

6. About 10 minutes before baking, preheat oven to 375 degrees.

7. Bake for 25 minutes or until the internal temperature of the loaves reaches 190 degrees.

8. Immediately remove bread from pans and cool on a rack.

Bits & Pieces

Bananas can be stored in the refrigerator. Their skins turn yucky brown, but the fruit inside is fine.

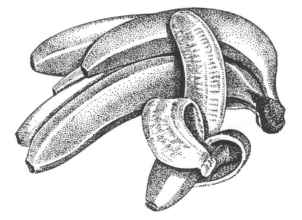

Hearty Healthy Loaf

Makes 2 Loaves

*This is a very hearty loaf. Take care not to add too much flour.
You could end up with a Heavy Hearty Healthy Loaf! When you
eat a hearty loaf, it will hug you from the inside out, but a heavy
loaf will sit in the pit of your stomach like a brick!*

2 cups milk
½ cup honey
½ cup cracked wheat
2 scant tablespoons or 2 (¼-ounce) packages active dry yeast
½ cup warm water (about 110 degrees)
½ cup shredded coconut
2 teaspoons salt
3 tablespoons soy flour (optional)
¼ cup wheat germ
½ cup unprocessed bran
½ cup sunflower seeds
4½ to 5½ cups unbleached flour

1. Heat the milk and honey until just before it boils. Remove
   from heat, add the cracked wheat, cover and cool to 110
   degrees.

2. In a large bowl, stir yeast into water to soften. Add the milk-
   honey mixture, coconut, salt, soy flour, wheat germ, bran,
   sunflower seeds, and 2 cups flour. Beat vigorously for two
   minutes.

3. Gradually add flour, ¼ cup at a time, until the dough begins
   to pull away from the side of the bowl.

4. Turn dough out onto a floured work surface. Knead, adding
   flour a little at a time, until you have a smooth, elastic dough.

5. Put dough into an oiled bowl. Turn to coat the entire ball of dough with oil. Cover with a tightly woven towel and let rise until doubled, about one hour.

6. Turn the dough out onto a lightly oiled work surface and divide in half. Shape each half into a loaf and place into well-greased loaf pans. Cover with a tightly woven towel and let rise until almost doubled, about 45 minutes.

7. About 10 minutes before baking, preheat oven to 375 degrees.

8. Bake for 25 minutes, or until the internal temperature of the loaves reaches 190 degrees.

9. Immediately remove bread from pans and cool on a rack.

Bits & Pieces

"We take out the germ and nourishment of the wheat and feed it to the pigs and keep the rubbish for ourselves. Who would ever think of trying to fatten a pig on white flour?"...H. S. Joyce, *I was Born in the Country, 1946.*

Anise Orange Nut Rye Bread

Makes 2 Loaves

This is a full-bodied bread with strong, bold flavors and textures. Crushing the anise seeds with a mortar and pestle, or by gently pounding with a hammer on a cutting board, releases their licorice flavor.

2 scant tablespoons or 2 (¼-ounce) packages active dry yeast
½ cup warm water (about 110 degrees)
2 cups warm milk (about 110 degrees)
½ cup honey
2 cups rye flour
¼ cup vegetable oil
2 teaspoons salt
1 tablespoon grated orange peel
2 teaspoons crushed anise seed
1 cup coarsely chopped walnuts
4 to 6 cups unbleached flour
Additional Oil (optional)

1. In a large bowl, stir yeast into water to soften. Add milk, honey, rye flour, oil, salt, orange peel, anise seed, walnuts, and 1 cup unbleached flour. Beat vigorously for two minutes.

2. Gradually add flour, ¼ cup at a time, until the dough begins to pull away from the side of the bowl.

3. Turn dough out onto a floured work surface. Knead, adding flour a little at a time, until you have a smooth, elastic dough.

4. Put dough into an oiled bowl. Turn to coat the entire ball of dough with oil. Cover with a tightly woven towel and let rise until doubled, about one hour.

5. Turn the dough out onto a lightly oiled work surface and divide in half. Shape each half into a ball and place on a well-greased baking sheet. Flatten the top slightly. Cover with a tightly woven towel and let rise until almost doubled, about 45 minutes.

6. About 10 minutes before baking, preheat oven to 375 degrees.

7. Just before baking, slit the top of each loaf into a diamond pattern (see loaf below).

8. Bake for 25 minutes, or until the internal temperature of the loaves reaches 190 degrees.

9. Immediately remove loaves from pans and cool on a rack.

10. For a soft, shiny crust, brush top of each loaf with oil.

Beer Rye Bread

Makes 2 Loaves

This bread has an unusually bitter, but robust taste. Pour the beer into a container and let it go flat. If you add salt to beer that isn't flat, it will foam and triple in size. Try serving the bread the European style - sliced thinly, spread with butter with thin slices of sweet onion or lightly salted slices of Emmenthal cheese.

2 scant tablespoons or 2 (¼-ounce) packages active dry yeast
½ cup warm water (about 110 degrees)
2 cups flat beer (the darker the better)
2 tablespoons vegetable oil
2 teaspoons granulated sugar
2 cups rye flour
2 teaspoons salt
2 tablespoons caraway seeds
4 to 5 cups unbleached flour
Cornmeal (optional)

1. In a large bowl, stir yeast into water to soften. Add beer, oil, sugar, rye flour, salt, caraway seeds, and 2 cups unbleached flour. Beat vigorously for two minutes.

2. Gradually add flour, ¼ cup at a time, until the dough begins to pull away from the side of the bowl.

3. Turn dough out onto a floured work surface. Knead, adding flour a little at a time, until you have a smooth, elastic dough.

4. Put dough into an oiled bowl. Turn to coat the entire ball of dough with oil. Cover with a tightly woven towel and let rise until doubled, about one hour.

5. Turn the dough out onto a lightly oiled work surface and divide in half. Shape each half into a ball and place on a well-greased baking sheet. Flatten the top of the loaves slightly.

Cover with a tightly woven towel and let rise until almost doubled, about 45 minutes.

6. About 10 minutes before baking, preheat oven to 375 degrees.

7. Bake for 25 minutes, or until the internal temperature of the loaf reaches 190 degrees.

8. Immediately remove bread from baking sheet and cool on a rack.

Black Peasant Bread

Makes 2 Loaves

This recipe produces a whole-bodied, rough-textured bread. I use blackstrap molasses, which gives the bread a slightly bitter taste (great served with cheeses). I also like to cut this bread into chunks to use with cheese fondue...yum!

2 scant tablespoons or 2 (¼-ounce) packages active dry yeast
1½ cups warm water (about 110 degrees)
¼ cup vegetable oil
½ cup molasses
2 tablespoons caraway seeds
2 teaspoons salt
½ cup wheat germ
¼ cup cocoa powder
2 cups rye flour
5½ to 6½ cups unbleached flour
Cornmeal (optional)
Butter (optional)

1. In a large bowl, stir yeast into water to soften. Add oil, molasses, caraway seeds, salt, wheat germ, cocoa powder, rye flour and 1 cup unbleached flour. Beat vigorously for two minutes.

2. Gradually add flour, ¼ cup at a time, until the dough begins to pull away from the side of the bowl.

3. Turn dough out onto a floured work surface. Knead, adding flour a little at a time, until you have a smooth, elastic dough.

4. Put dough into an oiled bowl. Turn to coat the entire ball of dough with oil. Cover with a tightly woven towel and let rise until doubled, about one hour.

5.   Turn dough out onto a lightly oiled work surface and divide in half. Shape each half into a round ball and place on a well-greased baking sheet that has been sprinkled with cornmeal (makes bottom crust crisper). Flatten the top of the loaves slightly. Cover with a tightly woven towel and let rise until almost doubled, about 45 minutes.

6.   About 10 minutes before baking, preheat oven to 375 degrees.

7.   Just before baking, slit the top of each loaf in two or three places about ¼-inch deep.

8.   Bake for 25 minutes or until the internal temperature of the loaves reaches 190 degrees.

9.   Immediately remove bread from baking sheet and cool on a rack.

10. For a softer, shinier crust, rub the tops of the loaves with butter while still warm.

Bits & Pieces

Many peasants would grate their stale bread and add it back into the next recipe of bread. The nutrients in stale bread amount to nil, but the flavor is outstanding!

Buttermilk Rye Baguettes

Makes 2 Loaves

Baguettes are long cylindrical loaves baked either freestanding on a baking sheet or in a baguette pan (looks like a small stovepipe cut in half lengthwise). (If you don't have a baguette pan, use a baking sheet or two 8½ by 4½-inch loaf pans.)

2 scant tablespoons or 2 (¼-ounce) packages active dry yeast
½ cup warm water (about 110 degrees)
1½ cups warm buttermilk (about 110 degrees)
2 tablespoons vegetable oil
3 tablespoons molasses
1 tablespoon caraway seeds
2 teaspoons salt
1½ cups rye flour
3½ to 4½ cups unbleached flour
Glaze - 1 egg beaten with 1 tablespoon cold water

1. In a large bowl, stir yeast into water to soften. Add buttermilk, oil, molasses, caraway seeds, salt, rye flour, and 1 cup unbleached flour. Beat vigorously for two minutes.

2. Gradually add flour, ¼ cup at a time, until the dough begins to pull away from the side of the bowl.

3. Turn dough out onto a floured work surface. Knead, adding flour a little at a time, until you have a smooth, elastic dough.

4. Put dough into an oiled bowl. Turn to coat the entire ball of dough with oil. Cover with a tightly woven towel and let rise until doubled, about one hour.

5. Turn the dough out onto a lightly oiled work surface and divide in half. Roll each half with a rolling pin into a 10 by 15-inch oval. Roll up into a 15-inch cylinder. Pinch seams to seal and taper the ends slightly. Place seam-side down on

well-greased baguette pans or baking sheet. Cover with a tightly woven towel and let rise until almost doubled, about 45 minutes.

6. About 10 minutes before baking, preheat the oven to 400 degrees.

7. Just before baking, slit each loaf diagonally about ¼ inch deep in 3 or 4 places. Lightly brush the top of each baguette with the glaze.

8. Bake for 20 minutes or until the internal temperature of the loaves reaches 190 degrees.

9. Immediately remove bread from pans and cool on a rack.

Bits & Pieces

Does your bread go stale before you can use a whole loaf? Divide the loaf into two balls then put both balls in a standard loaf pan end-to-end. After they've cooled, pull the sections apart to use as short loaves.

Caraway Rye Bread

Makes 2 Loaves

If you love the flavor of rye and caraway seeds as much as I do, you'll be making this recipe often. To keep the loaves from coming out like rocks, make sure the dough is sticky at the end of the kneading process.

2 scant tablespoons or 2 (¼-ounce) packages active dry yeast
2½ cups warm water (about 110 degrees)
2 tablespoons vegetable shortening
¼ cup molasses
2 teaspoons salt
2 tablespoons caraway seeds
2 cups rye flour
3½ to 4½ cups unbleached flour

1. In a large bowl, stir yeast into water to soften. Add shortening, molasses, salt, caraway seeds, rye flour, and 2 cups unbleached flour. Beat vigorously for two minutes.

2. Gradually add flour, ¼ cup at a time, until the dough begins to pull away from the side of the bowl.

3. Turn dough out onto a floured work surface. Knead, adding flour a little at a time, until you have a smooth, elastic dough.

4. Put dough into an oiled bowl. Turn to coat the entire ball of dough with oil. Cover with a tightly woven towel and let rise until doubled, about one hour.

5. Turn dough out onto a lightly oiled work surface and divide in half. Shape each half into a ball and place onto a well-greased baking sheet. Flatten the top of the loaves slightly. Cover with a tightly woven towel and let rise until almost doubled, about 45 minutes.

6. About 10 minutes before baking, preheat oven to 375 degrees.

7. Slit the top of each loaf in two or three places about ¼-inch deep. Brush each loaf lightly with cold water.

8. Bake for 25 minutes or until the internal temperature of the loaves reaches 190 degrees.

9. Immediately remove bread from baking sheet and cool on a rack.

Cinnamon Raisin Pumpernickel Bread

Makes 2 Round Loaves

This bread consists of a hearty combination of flours with cinnamon and raisins. The soy flour is added as a conditioner to keep the texture light. The sweet flavor of this bread especially complements cheeses, but is also marvelous used for sandwiches.

2 scant tablespoons or 2 (¼-ounce) packages active dry yeast
2½ cups warm water (about 110 degrees)
½ cup molasses
¼ cup cocoa
¼ cup soft butter
2 teaspoons salt
2 tablespoons cinnamon
2 cups raisins
1 cup rye flour
1 cup whole wheat flour
3 tablespoons soy flour (optional)
½ cup unprocessed bran
3 to 4 cups unbleached flour

1. In a large bowl, stir yeast into water to soften. Add molasses, cocoa, butter, salt, cinnamon, raisins, rye flour, whole wheat flour, soy flour, bran, and 1 cup unbleached flour. Beat vigorously for two minutes.

2. Gradually add flour, ¼ cup at a time, until the dough begins to pull away from the side of the bowl.

3. Turn dough out onto a floured work surface. Knead, adding flour a little at a time, until you have a smooth, elastic dough.

4. Put dough into an oiled bowl. Turn to coat the entire ball of dough with oil. Cover with a tightly woven towel and let rise until doubled, about one hour.

5. Turn dough out onto a lightly oiled work surface and divide in half. Shape each half into a ball and place onto a well-greased baking sheet. Flatten the top of the loaves slightly. Cover with a tightly woven towel and let rise until almost doubled, about 45 minutes.

6. About 10 minutes before baking, preheat oven to 375 degrees.

7. Just before baking, slit the top of each loaf in a tic-tac-toe pattern about ¼-inch deep.

8. Bake for 25 minutes or until the internal temperature of the loaves reaches 190 degrees.

9. Immediately remove bread from baking sheet and cool on a rack.

Bits & Pieces

Did you know that when the truth-in-advertising laws went into effect, the Food and Drug Administration tried to have soy milk renamed because it didn't come from mammary glands? Soy milk is available in health food stores and is an ideal liquid to use in yeast breads. Soy conditions dough and is very nutritious. It can be substituted for milk or water in any recipe.

Mustard Seed Rye Bread

Makes 2 Loaves

Rye breads make marvelous sandwiches and this pungent mustard flavored bread is no exception. Try serving this the European style - sliced thinly, spread with butter and topped with thin slices of sweet onion.

2 scant tablespoons or 2 (¼-ounce) packages active dry yeast
2½ cups warm water (about 110 degrees)
¼ cup grainy prepared mustard
2 teaspoons salt
1 tablespoon granulated sugar
2 tablespoons mustard seeds
2 cups rye flour
4 to 5 cups unbleached flour
Cornmeal (optional)
Olive oil (optional)

1. In a large mixing bowl, stir yeast into water to soften. Add mustard, salt, sugar, mustard seeds, rye flour, and 1 cup unbleached flour. Beat vigorously for two minutes.

2. Gradually add flour, ¼ cup at a time, until the dough begins to pull away from the side of the bowl.

3. Turn dough out onto a floured work surface. Knead, adding flour a little at a time, until you have a smooth, elastic dough.

4. Put dough into an oiled bowl. Turn to coat the entire ball of dough with oil. Cover with a tightly woven towel and let rise until doubled, about one hour.

5. Turn the dough out onto a lightly oiled work surface and divide in half. Shape each half into a ball and place on a well-greased baking sheet that has been sprinkled with cornmeal. Flatten the top of the loaves slightly. Cover with a

tightly woven towel and let rise until almost doubled, about 45 minutes.

6. About 10 minutes before baking, preheat oven to 375 degrees.

7. Just before baking, slit the top of each loaf with an "x" about ¾-inch deep and brush the loaves lightly with olive oil.

8. Bake for 25 minutes, or until the internal temperature of the loaves reaches 190 degrees.

9. Immediately remove bread from baking sheet and cool on a rack.

Rolls, Bagels & Buns

No-Knead Parkerhouse Rolls

Parkerhouse Rolls became famous at the Parkerhouse Hotel in Boston. On a trip to Boston, I attended a meeting with my friend, June Jacobs, who told me the following limerick. I seem to have gotten credit for the limerick since my food friends frequently want me to tell them "my" limerick about the Parkerhouse Rolls! When I was in Atlanta, I even received a bouquet of flowers addressed to the "Parkerhouse Roll Lady."

> THERE ONCE WAS A WOMAN FROM KROLL,
> WHO IN HER SENSE OF HUMOR WAS QUITE DROLL,
> SHE WENT TO A MASQUERADE BALL,
> DRESSED IN NOTHING AT ALL,
> AND BACKED IN AS A PARKERHOUSE ROLL.

2 scant tablespoons or 2 ($\frac{1}{4}$-ounce) packages active dry yeast
$\frac{1}{2}$ cup warm water (about 110 degrees)
2 cups warm milk (about 110 degrees)
2 large eggs
$\frac{1}{2}$ cup soft butter
2 teaspoons salt
$\frac{1}{2}$ cup granulated sugar
$6\frac{1}{2}$ cups unbleached flour
$\frac{1}{2}$ cup melted butter

1. In a large bowl, stir yeast into water to soften. Add milk, eggs, butter, salt, sugar and 3 cups flour. Beat vigorously for two minutes.

2. Gradually add flour, $\frac{1}{4}$ cup at a time, beating well after each addition. Brush the top of the dough with oil, lay a piece of plastic wrap on the dough, and cover the plastic wrap with a tightly woven towel. Refrigerate for 2 to 24 hours.

3. Turn the dough out onto a floured work surface (yes, I know we've used oil in every recipe, but we need the flour to help keep the fold in middle of the rolls). With a rolling pin, roll dough to about ¼-inch thickness. Cut out with a 2-inch round cutter. Stretch the dough slightly into a 2 by 2 ½-inch oval. Dip one side of each roll into melted butter and fold the roll in half with the butter on the outside and the flour on the inside. Place on well-greased baking sheets about ½-inch apart. Cover with a tightly woven towel and let rise until almost doubled, about 45 minutes.

4. About 10 minutes before baking, preheat oven to 400 degrees.

5. Bake for 15 minutes, or until the internal temperature of the rolls reaches 190 degrees.

6. Immediately remove rolls from pans and cool on a rack.

Apple Cider Cinnamon Cloverleaf Rolls

Makes 36 Rolls

I think about these rolls in the fall when the cider presses are turning out fresh, robust tasting cider and the air is crisp and cool. Though the cloverleaf shape is a bit more time consuming to make, I love the shape. They can be shaped into a basic round roll if you prefer.

2 scant tablespoons or 2 (¼-ounce) packages active dry yeast
½ cup warm water (about 110 degrees)
2 cups warm apple cider (about 110 degrees)
½ cup firmly packed brown sugar
2 teaspoons salt
2 cups finely chopped tart apples, pared and cored
1 teaspoon cinnamon
6½ to 7½ cups unbleached flour
Glaze - 1 egg beaten with 1 tablespoon cold water

1. In a large bowl, stir yeast into water to soften. Add cider, sugar, salt, apples, cinnamon, and 3 cups flour. Beat vigorously for two minutes.

2. Gradually add flour, ¼ cup at a time, until the dough begins to pull away from the side of the bowl.

3. Turn dough out onto a floured work surface. Knead, adding flour a little at a time, until you have a smooth, elastic dough.

4. Put dough into an oiled bowl. Turn to coat the entire ball of dough with oil. Cover with a tightly woven towel and let rise until doubled, about one hour.

5. Turn the dough out onto a lightly oiled work surface and divide into 108 pieces. Shape each piece into a ball. Place three balls together to form a triangle. Pinch the balls together from the top. Pick them up, turn them over and

circle them with your thumb and index finger squeezing them together slightly so they will easily fit into a well-greased muffin pan. Cover with a tightly woven towel and let rise until almost doubled, about 45 minutes.

6. About 10 minutes before baking, preheat oven to 400 degrees.

7. Just before baking, brush each roll lightly with the glaze.

8. Bake for 15 minutes, or until the internal temperature of the rolls reaches 190 degrees.

9. Immediately remove rolls from pans and cool on a rack.

Ensaymadas

48 Large Rolls

These Philippine rolls are much like brioche, but the sprinkling of sugar on top before baking makes Ensaymadas unique. It takes a long time to make these, and if you try to short cut any of the steps, you'll sacrifice the quality of the finished product!

2 scant tablespoons or 2 (¼-ounce) packages active dry yeast
1 cup warm water (about 110 degrees)
6 to 7 cups unbleached flour, *divided*
8 egg yolks
1 cup sugar, *divided*
¾ cup soft butter
3 cups grated Edam cheese, *divided*
¾ cup melted butter, *divided*
Granulated sugar

1. In a large bowl, stir yeast into water to soften. Add *2 cups flour*, stir, cover with a tightly woven towel and let rise until doubled, about one hour.

2. Add egg yolks, *¾ cup sugar* and soft butter to flour mixture and mix. Gradually add flour, ¼ cup at a time, beating well after each addition. Cover and let rise until doubled, about 3 hours.

3. Turn the dough out onto a lightly oiled work surface and divide in fourths. Shape each piece into a ball. Cover with a tightly woven towel and let rest 5 minutes.

4. Roll each ball of dough with a rolling pin into a 12-inch circle, brush the dough with *melted butter* and sprinkle *½ cup cheese* on **EACH** round. Cut each round into 12 wedges. Starting with the wide end, roll up each piece. Place on parchment-lined baking sheets making sure the point is on the underside. Turn the ends of the dough toward the center

to form a crescent shape. Cover and let rise until doubled, about 4 hours.

5. About 10 minutes before baking, preheat oven to 350 degrees.

6. Bake for 15 minutes, or until lightly browned. Brush rolls with remaining *melted butter*, sprinkle with *remaining cheese*, and granulated sugar. Return to oven for 2 minutes.

7. Immediately remove roll from baking sheets and cool on a rack. Best served warm.

Knotted Onion Sage Rolls

Makes 36 Rolls

Because of the favorable chemical reaction between onions and yeast, onions are known as a "friend of yeast." Whenever "a friend" is used, you can expect more volume, and a moister texture. This bread makes terrific loaves for sandwiches.

2 cups finely chopped onions
2 tablespoons olive oil
2 scant tablespoons or 2 (¼-ounce) packages active dry yeast
½ cup warm water (about 110 degrees)
2 cups warm milk (about 110 degrees)
¼ cup vegetable shortening
¼ cup honey
2 teaspoons salt
5 to 6 cups unbleached flour
2 tablespoons rubbed fresh sage or 2 teaspoons rubbed dried sage
1½ cups whole wheat flour
Olive oil (optional)

1. Sauté onions in olive oil until soft, but not brown. Set aside and cool.

2. In a large bowl, stir yeast into water to soften. Add milk, shortening, honey, salt, 2 cups flour, and cooled onions. Beat vigorously for two minutes.

3. Whisk sage and whole wheat flour together and add to onion mixture. Stir to incorporate.

4. Gradually add flour, ¼ cup at a time, until the dough begins to pull away from the side of the bowl.

5. Turn dough out onto a floured work surface. Knead, adding flour a little at a time, until you have a smooth, elastic dough.

6.   Put dough into an oiled bowl. Turn to coat the entire ball of dough with oil. Cover with a tightly woven towel and let rise until doubled, about one hour.

7.   Turn the dough out onto a lightly oiled work surface and divide into 36 equal pieces. Shape each piece into an 8-inch strand and tie it into a single knot. Place about three inches apart on parchment-lined baking sheets. (These knotted rolls are also attractive if placed into well-greased muffin pans.) Cover with a tightly woven towel and let rise until almost doubled, about 45 minutes.

8.   About 10 minutes before baking, preheat oven to 400 degrees.

9.   Bake for 15 minutes, or until the internal temperature of the rolls reaches 190 degrees.

10.   Immediately remove rolls from baking sheets and cool on a rack.

11.   For a shiny, soft crust, brush the tops of the rolls with olive oil.

Onion Poppy Seed Rolls

Makes 36 Rolls or 18 Large Buns

*Certain tastes and textures just naturally seem to go together.
Onion and poppy seeds fall into that category for me. These rolls
are light and airy which make them perfect as a dinner roll. The
sweet onions become gutsy tasting when joined with ground beef
which makes them an excellent hamburger bun.*

2 cups finely minced onions
4 tablespoons olive oil, *divided*
2 scant tablespoons or 2 (¼-ounce) packages active dry yeast
½ cup warm water (about 110 degrees)
2 cups warm milk (about 110 degrees)
2 tablespoons granulated sugar
2 teaspoons salt
1 teaspoon celery seeds
2 tablespoons poppy seeds
5½ to 6½ unbleached flour

1. Sauté onions in *2 tablespoons of oil* until soft, but not brown.
   Set aside and cool.

2. In a large bowl, stir yeast into water to soften. Add *remaining
   oil*, milk, sugar, salt, celery seeds, poppy seeds, cooled onions,
   and 2 cups flour. Beat vigorously for two minutes.

3. Gradually add flour, ¼ cup at a time, until the dough begins
   to pull away from the side of the bowl.

4. Turn dough out onto a floured work surface. Knead, adding
   flour a little at a time, until you have a smooth, elastic dough.

5. Put dough into an oiled bowl. Turn to coat the entire ball of
   dough with oil. Cover with a tightly woven towel and let rise
   until doubled, about one hour.

6. Turn dough out onto a lightly oiled work surface and divide into 36 pieces (18 for hamburger buns). Shape each piece into a ball and flatten to about ½-inch thick. Place about 3 inches apart on well-greased baking sheets*. Cover with a tightly woven towel and let rise until almost doubled, about 45 minutes.

7. About 10 minutes before baking, preheat oven to 400 degrees.

8. Bake rolls for 15 minutes, buns for 20 minutes, or until the internal temperature reaches 190 degrees.

9. Immediately remove rolls from baking sheets and cool on a rack.

*For soft-sided buns, place ½-inch apart on the baking sheet so they will grow together as they rise.

Bits & Pieces

Most any loaf recipe can be shaped into rolls and most any roll recipe can be shaped into loaves.

Bagels

Makes 32 Bagels

Bagels were made famous by early Jewish immigrants who sold them on the streets of New York City. Bagels are doughnut shaped, but the center almost grows back together. These bagels are refrigerated for 12 to 24 hours, which gives time for the flavors to develop. If you're in a hurry, you can leave them at room temperature and let them rise for 30 minutes. However, the longer version produces a more flavorful bagel with a firmer crust. Poaching in sugar water before baking gives them a wonderful soft-textured inside with a very chewy crust. These are marvelous spread with cream cheese, then layered with thin slices of lox (smoked salmon), thinly sliced ripe tomatoes, and onions.

2 scant tablespoons or 2 (¼-ounce) packages active dry yeast
2½ cups warm water (about 110 degrees)
2 teaspoons salt
2 tablespoons barley malt syrup or powder (see "Sources" on
   page 183)
7 to 8 cups unbleached flour
Cornmeal for dusting pans
2 tablespoons granulated sugar
2 quarts boiling water
Glaze ~ 1 egg beaten with 2 tablespoons milk
Poppy, Sesame, Coarse Salt or Caraway Seeds (optional)

1.   In a large bowl, stir yeast into water to soften. Add salt, barley malt, and 4 cups flour. Beat vigorously for two minutes.

2.   Gradually add flour, ¼ cup at a time, until the dough begins to pull away from the side of the bowl.

3.   Turn dough out onto a floured work surface. Knead, adding flour a little at a time, until you have a smooth, elastic

dough. Bagel dough should be kneaded for at least 15 minutes. Add enough flour to make the dough stand in a firm ball on the work surface (should be more firm than regular bread dough).

4. Put dough into an oiled bowl. Turn to coat the entire ball of dough with oil. Cover with a tightly woven towel and let rise until doubled, about one hour.

5. Turn the dough out onto a lightly oiled work surface. Divide into 32 equal pieces of dough. Shape each piece into a ball. Insert your finger or thumb through the center of each ball and stretch to make a 1½-inch hole. Place on baking sheets that have been lightly sprinkled with cornmeal. Cover lightly with plastic wrap then a tightly woven tightly woven towel. Both covers are essential! Refrigerate for 12 to 24 hours.

6. About 10 minutes before baking, preheat oven to 400 degrees. Remove the bagels from the refrigerator.

7. In a 12-inch Dutch-style oven or large cooking vessel, dissolve the sugar in the boiling water. Keep the water on a slow boil.

8. Drop three or four bagels, one at a time, into the water. *Do not crowd.* Turn them over and simmer for three minutes. Remove with a slotted spoon. Place upside down on a well-greased or parchment-lined baking sheet. Turning them upside down (the upside is the one that was under the water the longest) produces a better crust.

9. Just before baking, brush each bagel lightly with the glaze and sprinkle with seeds or salt, if desired.

10. Bake for 20 minutes, or until browned.

11. Immediately remove bagels from baking sheets and cool on a rack.

Wheat Berry Buns

Makes 24 Buns

Whole wheat berries are quite common in Scandinavian Breads. I love texture in my bread and often add cooked whole berries to basic doughs. This particular bread will have a wonderfully light, yet robust flavor if you do not add too much flour. Use these buns for hamburgers or sandwiches.

½ cup wheat berries or kernels
2 cups boiling water
2 scant tablespoons or 2 (¼-ounce) packages active dry yeast
2½ cups warm water (about 110 degrees)
½ cup brown sugar, firmly packed
2 teaspoons salt
½ cup unprocessed bran
6½ to 7½ cups unbleached flour

1. Add wheat berries to the boiling water. Turn the heat to low, cover the pan, and allow to simmer for 15 minutes. Turn off the heat, leave covered, and allow to cool, about 1½ hours. Drain.

2. In a large bowl, stir yeast into the warm water to soften. Add the wheat berries, brown sugar, salt, bran and 3 cups flour. Beat vigorously for two minutes.

3. Gradually add flour, ¼ cup at a time, until the dough begins to pull away from the side of the bowl.

4. Turn dough out onto a floured work surface. Knead, adding flour a little at a time, until you have a smooth, elastic dough.

5. Put dough into an oiled bowl. Turn to coat the entire ball of dough with oil. Cover with a tightly woven towel and let rise until doubled, about one hour.

6. Turn dough out onto a lightly oiled work surface and divide into 24 pieces. Shape each piece into a ball, cover with a tightly woven towel, and let rest on the work surface for 5 minutes. Flatten each ball to about ½-inch thick. Place buns about ½-inch apart on a well-greased baking sheet. Cover with a tightly woven towel and let rise until almost doubled, about 45 minutes.

7. About 10 minutes before baking, preheat oven to 400 degrees.

8. Bake for 20 minutes, or until the internal temperature of the buns reaches 190 degrees.

9. Immediately remove buns from baking sheet and cool on a rack.

Bits & Pieces

Never use plastic bags from the produce section of your supermarket for bread storage. The bags have minuscule holes in them which let fruits and vegetables breathe, but which dry out baked goods quickly.

10-Grain Rolls

Makes 36 Rolls

See page 77 for 10-Grain Mix recipe or you may purchase a multi-grain cereal mix in health food stores. The walnuts complement the mixture of grains for a full-bodied roll. These can also be shaped into 18 buns for hamburgers or sandwiches.

1 cup 10-grain mix
2 cups boiling water
2 scant tablespoons or 2 (¼-ounce) packages active dry yeast
½ cup warm water (about 110 degrees)
¼ cup vegetable oil
¼ cup brown sugar, firmly packed
2 teaspoons salt
4½ to 5½ cups unbleached flour
1 cup coarsely chopped walnuts, toasted

1. Add the 10-grain mix to the boiling water, cover, cool to 110 degrees.

2. In a large bowl, stir yeast into warm water to soften. Add cooled grain mix, oil, brown sugar, salt, 2 cups flour, and walnuts. Beat vigorously for two minutes.

3. Gradually add flour, ¼ cup at a time, until the dough begins to pull away from the side of the bowl.

4. Turn dough out onto a floured work surface. Knead, adding flour a little at a time, until you have a smooth, elastic dough.

5. Put dough into an oiled bowl. Turn to coat the entire ball of dough with oil. Cover with a tightly woven towel and let rise until doubled, about one hour.

6. Turn the dough out onto a lightly oiled work surface and divide into 36 pieces. Shape each piece into a ball and place

about 3 inches apart, on well-greased baking sheets. Cover with a tightly woven towel and let rise until almost doubled, about 45 minutes.

7. About 10 minutes before baking, preheat oven to 400 degrees.

8. Bake for 15 minutes, or until the internal temperature of the rolls reaches 190 degrees.

9. Immediately remove rolls from baking sheets and cool on a rack.

Crusty Semolina Rolls

Semolina flour is made from durum wheat and is primarily used for making pasta. I love the nutty taste semolina flour imparts in breads. These crisp rolls are a wonderful addition to any meal. They also make great sandwich rolls.

2 scant tablespoons or 2 (¼-ounce) packages active dry yeast
2½ cups warm water (about 110 degrees)
2 tablespoons granulated sugar
2 teaspoons salt
2 tablespoons olive oil
5½ to 6½ cups semolina flour
3 stiffly beaten egg whites
Cornmeal (optional)
Glaze - 1 egg beaten until slightly frothy with 1 teaspoon salt

1. In a large bowl, stir yeast into water to soften. Add sugar, salt, olive oil, and 2 cups flour. Beat vigorously for two minutes. Fold in egg whites and continue to stir until they are completely mixed into the dough - be patient, this make take a couple of minutes.

2. Gradually add flour, ¼ cup at a time, until the dough begins to pull away from the side of the bowl.

3. Turn dough out onto a floured work surface. Knead, adding flour a little at a time, until you have a smooth, elastic dough.

4. Put dough into an oiled bowl. Turn to coat the entire ball of dough with oil. Cover with a tightly woven towel and let rise until doubled, about one hour.

5. Turn the dough out onto a lightly oiled work surface and divide into 28 pieces. Shape each piece into a ball, then roll each one into a 4-inch long cylinder. Place 3 inches apart on

well-greased baking sheets that have been sprinkled with cornmeal. Cover with a tightly woven towel and let rise until almost doubled, about 45 minutes.

6. About 10 minutes before baking, preheat oven to 400 degrees.

7. Just before baking, make a ½-inch slit from end to end across the top of each roll and brush lightly with the glaze.

8. Bake for 20 minutes, or until the internal temperature of the rolls reaches 190 degrees.

9. Immediately remove rolls from baking sheets and cool on a rack.

NOTE: I PREFER TO USE A STONE TO BAKE THESE ROLLS. BAKING ON A STONE GIVES AN EXTRA CRISPY CRUST. LET THE ROLLS RISE ON BAKING SHEETS. PREHEAT THE BAKING STONE FOR 30 MINUTES, THEN CAREFULLY LIFT THE ROLLS FROM THE BAKING SHEET AND PLACE THEM DIRECTLY ON THE STONE. THEY WILL BAKE IN THE SAME AMOUNT OF TIME AT THE SAME TEMPERATURE.

Maple Cornmeal Rolls

Makes 36 rolls

*These hearty rolls go well with any type of meal, especially soups
and stews. They have a slightly sweet flavor that helps bring out
the flavors of the foods served with them. Cornmeal, ground
from dried whole kernels of yellow or white corn, is sold as
stone-ground or enriched-degerminated (sometimes called
bolted). Stone-ground cornmeal is more nutritious because it still
contains the germ. It has a rich, intense corn flavor and oily
quality, which imparts a sweet crunchy taste and texture to
breads. Breads made with degerminated cornmeal tend to have
dry crumbly texture.*

2 scant tablespoons or 2 (¼-ounce) packages active dry yeast
2½ cups warm water (about 110 degrees)
½ cup maple syrup
2 teaspoons salt
¼ cup vegetable shortening
1½ cups stone-ground cornmeal
4½ to 5½ cups unbleached flour

1. In a large bowl, stir yeast into water to soften. Add syrup,
    salt, shortening, cornmeal, and 2 cups flour. Beat vigorously
    for two minutes.

2. Gradually add flour, ¼ cup at a time, until the dough begins
    to pull away from the side of the bowl.

3. Turn dough out onto a floured work surface. Knead, adding
    flour a little at a time, until you have a smooth, elastic dough.

4. Put dough into an oiled bowl. Turn to coat the entire ball of
    dough with oil. Cover with a tightly woven towel and let rise
    until doubled, about one hour.

5. Turn the dough out onto a lightly oiled work surface and divide into 36 equal pieces. Shape each piece into a ball and place into well-greased muffin pans or a well-greased, 12-inch round pan with 2-inch sides (a deep dish pizza pan will work fine). Cover with a tightly woven towel and let rise until almost doubled, about 45 minutes.

6. About 10 minutes before baking, preheat oven to 400 degrees.

7. Bake for 15 minutes, or until the internal temperature of the rolls reaches 190 degrees.

8. Immediately remove rolls from pans and cool on a rack.

Bits & Pieces

Yeast, like man, luxuriates in warmer temperatures.

Wheat Germ 'n Honey Rolls

Makes 36 Rolls

These rolls are a little sweet which makes them especially suitable for breakfast or brunch. You can also shape them into 18 large sandwich buns. The sweet flavor blends nicely with tuna and chicken salads.

2 scant tablespoons or 2 (¼-ounce) packages active dry yeast
½ cup warm water (about 110 degrees)
2 cups warm milk (about 110 degrees)
¼ cup shortening
½ cup honey
2 teaspoons salt
1 cup wheat germ
5 to 6 cups unbleached flour

1. In a large bowl, stir yeast into water to soften. Add milk, shortening, honey, salt, wheat germ, and 2 cups flour. Beat vigorously for two minutes.

2. Gradually add flour, ¼ cup at a time, until the dough begins to pull away from the side of the bowl.

3. Turn dough out onto a floured work surface. Knead, adding flour a little at a time, until you have a smooth, elastic dough.

4. Put dough into an oiled bowl. Turn to coat the entire ball of dough with oil. Cover with a tightly woven towel and let rise until doubled, about one hour.

5. Turn dough out onto a lightly oiled work surface and divide into 36 pieces. Shape each piece into a ball. For soft rolls, place ½-inch apart on a well-greased baking sheet. For crispier rolls, place rolls in a well-greased muffin pan. Cover with a tightly woven towel and let rise until almost doubled, about 45 minutes.

6. About 10 minutes before baking, preheat oven to 400 degrees.

7. Bake for 15 minutes, or until the internal temperature of the rolls reaches 190 degrees.

8. Immediately remove rolls from baking sheet and cool on a rack.

Bits & Pieces

If you're not going to eat them right away, slightly undercook rolls and croissants. When you reheat them, you can brown them to finish the cooking process.

Specialty
Breads

Brioche

The classic French Brioche is a marvelous bread and well worth the extra effort involved to make it. It is probably one of the most difficult breads to make since the dough should be **extremely** *sticky (adding too much flour makes the dough heavy). Using a heavy-duty mixer helps solve this problem. If you don't have a heavy-duty mixer, use a dough scraper to toss and fold the dough in order to keep it from sticking to you, the work surface, or anything else it touches.*

2 scant tablespoons or 2 (¼-ounce) packages active dry yeast
¼ cup warm water (about 110 degrees)
2 tablespoons sugar
7 large eggs, room temperature
2 teaspoons salt
5 cups unbleached flour
1 cup soft butter
Glaze - 1 egg yolk beaten with 1 tablespoon cream

1. In a large bowl, stir yeast into water to soften. Add sugar, eggs, salt, and 3 cups of flour. Beat vigorously for two minutes.

2. Add butter, 1 tablespoon at a time, beating well after each addition. Add the remaining flour, ¼ cup at a time, beating well after each addition.

3. Beat the dough in a heavy-duty mixer for 10 minutes at medium-low speed **OR** work the dough by hand for 20 minutes by picking up the dough and slapping it down on a work surface over and over. The dough gets extremely sticky and this technique requires a lot of patience. Don't add more flour unless absolutely necessary.

4. Put the dough into a lightly oiled bowl and turn it once to make sure the entire ball is coated with oil. Cover with plastic wrap, then a tightly woven towel (this extra cover is necessary). Refrigerate the dough for at least 12 hours (the dough can be stored in the refrigerator for up to a week).

5. About two hours before baking, turn the dough out onto a lightly oiled work surface and cut off about ¼ of the dough. Shape this into a ball. Roll one side of the ball to turn it into a cone shape. Set aside.

6. Shape the remaining dough into a ball and place it into a well-greased brioche pan. With a well-oiled finger, punch a deep hole in the center of the large dough ball, going all the way to through the ball to the bottom of the pan. Insert the small end of the cone-shaped piece of dough into the hole (this keeps the top-notch in place when the dough rises and bakes).

7. Cover the Brioche lightly with plastic wrap and let rise for 1 hour and 45 minutes.

8. About 10 minutes before baking, preheat the oven to 375 degrees.

9. Just before baking, lightly brush the top of the Brioche with the glaze.

10. Bake for 40 minutes or until the internal temperature of the loaf reaches 190 degrees.

11. Immediately remove from pan and cool on a rack.

Variations:

Individual Brioche: Follow the instructions through Step 4. Divide dough in 24 equal pieces. Remove ¼ of each portion of dough and shape it into a ball. Roll one side of the ball to turn it into a cone shape. Set aside. Shape the remaining dough into balls and place them into well-greased individual ¾ cup brioche pans (see description of pans on page 12) or a muffin pan. With a well-oiled finger, punch a deep hole in the center of the large dough ball, going all the way to through the ball to the bottom of the pan. Insert the cone end of the first piece of dough into the hole (this keeps the top-notch in place when the dough rises and bakes). Continue at Step 7.

Cinnamon Buns: Follow the instructions through Step 4. Place dough between two sheets of plastic wrap and roll flat with a rolling pin making an 11 by 24-inch rectangle. Brush the surface of the dough lightly with melted butter, leaving a ½-inch strip along one long side of the rectangle free of butter. Sprinkle the dough evenly with 1 cup of firmly packed brown sugar and sprinkle liberally with ground cinnamon. Starting with the long edge opposite the unbuttered strip, roll up the dough into a 24-inch cylinder. Pinch the loose edge of the dough to the cylinder. Cut the cylinder into 24 1-inch slices (for easy cutting, see "Bits & Pieces" on page 167) and place cut-side up into a parchment-lined 9 by 13-inch pan. Continue at Step 7.

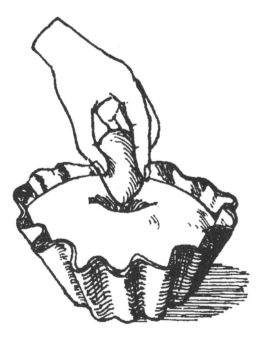

Focaccia

Makes 1 Large Flat Loaf

Focaccia (pronounced fo-ka-chee-ah) is gaining favor in America almost daily. There are so many variations of this bread that I could probably write a book on Focaccia alone. Listed below are a few variations. The garlic variation is my favorite. Don't be turned off by the fact that it calls for so much. When garlic is cooked slowly, much of the harsh pungency goes away, leaving a smooth buttery taste.

2 scant tablespoons or 2 (¼-ounce) packages active dry yeast
2 cups warm water (about 110 degrees)
½ cup olive oil, *divided*
2 teaspoons salt
2 tablespoons sugar
1 cup whole wheat flour
4½ to 5½ cups unbleached flour
Cornmeal (optional)
Coarse salt (optional – but it really makes a difference!)

1. In a large bowl, stir yeast into water to soften. Add *2 tablespoons olive oil*, salt, sugar, whole wheat flour, and 2 cups unbleached flour. Beat vigorously for two minutes.

2. Gradually add flour, ¼ cup at a time, until the dough begins to pull away from the side of the bowl.

3. Turn dough out onto a floured work surface. Knead, adding flour a little at a time, until you have a smooth, elastic dough.

4. Put dough into an oiled bowl. Turn to coat the entire ball of dough with oil. Cover with a tightly woven towel and let rise until doubled, about one hour.

5.   Grease a 13 by 18-inch baking sheet (with sides). For a crisper crust, sprinkle the baking sheet lightly with cornmeal.

6.   Turn dough out onto a lightly oiled work surface. Do not punch down or knead the dough or it will become elastic again. Using the heel of your hand, press the dough in to a rectangle as large as the baking sheet. Lift dough onto baking sheet and reshape if necessary. Cover with a tightly woven towel and let rise for 20 minutes.

7.   Dimple the dough with your fingertips, leaving ½-inch indentations to trap the pools of oil and salt that will cover the surface. Cover with a tightly woven towel and let rise for 20 minutes.

8.   About 10 minutes before baking, preheat oven to 375 degrees. Place a heavy pan on the bottom shelf of the oven.

9.   Just before baking, drizzle *remaining olive oil* over the surface of the dough and sprinkle with coarse salt.

10.   Place the dough in the oven and drop 5 ice cubes into the pan on the bottom shelf. Close the door quickly to prevent steam from escaping.

11.   Bake for 25 minutes, or until the internal temperature of the bread reaches 190 degrees.

12.   Immediately remove bread from baking sheet and cool on a rack.

Variations:

- **Seeded Focaccia** - Sprinkle the oiled and salted dough with sesame and/or poppy seeds just before baking.

- **Provolone Focaccia** - Cut 12 ounces of provolone cheese into ¼-inch cubes and knead into the dough just before shaping. This variation is good with or without salt.

- **Herbed Focaccia** - Sprinkle the oiled and salted dough with a liberal amount of fresh thyme, rosemary, oregano, or sage just before baking.

- **Garlic Focaccia** - Drizzle 4 heads (not cloves) of garlic with ¼ cup olive oil, season with salt and pepper. Roast in oven at 350 degrees until soft, about 45 minutes. Cool. Remove the skins, sliver, and sprinkle on the oiled and salted dough before baking.

- **Mozzarella Focaccia** - Combine ¼ cup heavy cream, 1 cup shredded mozzarella and ½ teaspoon oregano and spread over the oiled dough (no salt).

- **Olive Focaccia** - Pit and chop 8 ounces tart black olives, or a combination of black and green olives. Knead into the dough just before shaping.

Bits & Pieces

Why do Americans measure ingredients while most other cultures weigh them? American pioneers traveled across the country in wagons or on horseback. Scales were too heavy and bulky to carry. However, every pioneer had a drinking cup and spoon handy. If a small amount of an ingredient was used, they used a spoon to scoop it. If a large amount was used, they used a cup to scoop it.

Potato Focaccia

Makes 1 Large Flat Loaf

This focaccia is made with a potato dough which gives a soft velvety texture. It also has cooked potatoes as a topper. Though this bread is good at any time with most any food, I like to serve it with a crisp green salad for a delightful summertime supper.

2 medium russet potatoes
2 scant tablespoons or 2 (¼-ounce) packages active dry yeast
2 medium coarsely-grated raw russet potatoes
2 cloves minced garlic
2 teaspoons salt
2 tablespoons sugar
6 ½ to 7 ½ cups unbleached flour
Cornmeal, for sprinkling pans (optional)
Olive oil
1 tablespoon snipped fresh dill or 1 teaspoon dried dill
Coarse salt

1.   Put the two whole potatoes in a saucepan and cover with water. Bring to a boil and cook until potatoes are tender, about 20 minutes. Remove the potatoes from the water and set aside to cool. **Save the water for step 2.**

2.   In a large bowl, add yeast to 2 cups water that the potatoes were cooked in and stir to soften. Add grated potatoes, garlic, salt, sugar, and 2 cups unbleached flour and beat vigorously for two minutes.

3.   Gradually add flour, ¼ cup at a time, until the dough begins to pull away from the side of the bowl.

4.   Turn dough out onto a floured work surface. Knead, adding flour a little at a time, until you have a smooth, elastic dough.

5. Put dough into an oiled bowl. Turn to coat the entire ball of dough with oil. Cover with a tightly woven towel and let rise until doubled, about one hour.

6. Grease a 13 by 18-inch baking sheet (with sides). For a crisper crust, sprinkle the baking sheet lightly with cornmeal.

7. Turn dough out onto a lightly oiled work surface. Do not punch down or knead the dough or it will become elastic again. Using the heel of your hand, press the dough into a rectangle as large as the baking sheet. Lift dough onto baking sheet and reshape if necessary. Cover with a tightly woven towel and let rise for 20 minutes.

8. Slice the two cooled whole potatoes as thinly as possible (like potato chips). Spread the potatoes, overlapping slightly, over the top of the dough. Liberally brush the potatoes with olive oil. Cover with a tightly woven towel and let rise for 20 minutes.

9. About 10 minutes before baking, preheat oven to 375 degrees. Place a heavy pan on the bottom shelf of the oven.

10. Just before baking, rush the top of the bread once again with olive oil, sprinkle with dill and coarse salt.

11. Place the dough in the oven and drop 5 ice cubes into the pan on the bottom shelf. Close the door quickly to prevent steam from escaping.

12. Bake for 25 minutes, or until the internal temperature of the bread reaches 190 degrees.

13. Immediately remove bread from baking sheet and cool on a rack.

Nutty Breadsticks

Makes 48 Thick or 72 Thin Breadsticks

When making breadsticks, remember that dough doubles in size. I've seen folks shape the dough into the size they like and wind up being disappointed with the final product because the breadsticks are larger than they wanted. Breadsticks can be frozen and reheated in a 375-degree oven for ten minutes or until crispy.

2 scant tablespoons or 2 (¼-ounce) packages active dry yeast
2½ cups warm water (about 105 to 115 degrees)
2 tablespoons vegetable shortening
2 tablespoons granulated sugar
2 teaspoons salt
6 to 7 cups unbleached flour
1 cup finely chopped salted, roasted peanuts

1. In a large bowl, stir yeast into water to soften. Add shortening, sugar, salt, and 3 cups flour. Beat vigorously for two minutes.

2. Gradually add flour, ¼ cup at a time, until the dough begins to pull away from the side of the bowl.

3. Turn dough out onto a floured work surface. Knead, adding flour a little at a time, until you have a smooth, elastic dough.

4. Put dough into an oiled bowl. Turn to coat the entire ball of dough with oil. Cover with a tightly woven towel and let rise until doubled, about one hour.

5. Turn the dough out onto a lightly oiled work surface and divide into 48 pieces for thick breadsticks or 72 pieces if you prefer thinner ones. Roll each piece into a 10-inch long strand. Scatter the nuts over the work surface. Lightly roll the strand in the nuts so the strands become coated. Place on

well-greased baking sheets. Cover with a tightly woven towel and let rise until almost doubled, about 45 minutes.

6. About 10 minutes before baking, preheat oven to 400 degrees.

7. Bake thick breadsticks for 20 minutes, thin ones for 15 minutes.

8. Immediately remove breadsticks from baking sheets and cool on a rack.

NOTE: IF YOU PREFER EXTRA-CRISP BREADSTICKS, COOL THE OVEN TO 200 DEGREES. PUT BREADSTICKS BACK IN FOR 20 MINUTES MORE. THEY CAN BE BUNCHED ON THE BAKING SHEET AT THIS TIME.

Bits & Pieces

Sculpted breads can be traced back to 4000 years ago when Egyptian bakers baked bread into flower and bird shapes to use as offerings to the gods.

Millet Breadsticks

Makes 48 Thick Breadsticks or 72 Thin Breadsticks

You can serve these Italian Breadsticks as an hors d'oeuvre, with or without a dip, to accompany soups, or as a substitute for dinner rolls. They are also great to just nibble!

2½ cups boiling water
¾ cup millet
2 scant tablespoons or 2 (¼-ounce) packages active dry yeast
½ cup warm water (about 110 degrees)
2 tablespoons honey
2 tablespoons olive oil
2 teaspoons salt
5½ to 6½ cups unbleached flour
Olive oil (optional)

1. Pour boiling water over the millet in a large heatproof bowl. Cool to 110 degrees.

2. In a large bowl, stir yeast into water to soften. Add millet, honey, oil, salt, and 2 cups flour. Beat vigorously for two minutes.

3. Gradually add flour, ¼ cup at a time, until the dough begins to pull away from the side of the bowl.

4. Turn dough out onto a floured work surface. Knead, adding flour a little at a time, until you have a smooth, elastic dough.

5. Put dough into an oiled bowl. Turn to coat the entire ball of dough with oil. Cover with a tightly woven towel and let rise until doubled, about one hour.

6. Turn the dough out onto a lightly oiled work surface and divide into 48 (for thick sticks) or 72 (for thin sticks) equal

pieces. Shape each piece into a 10-inch strand and place about 1 inch apart on well-greased baking sheets. Cover with a tightly woven towel and let rise until almost doubled, about 45 minutes.

7. About 10 minutes before baking, preheat oven to 400 degrees.

8. For crispier bread sticks, brush the tops lightly with olive oil just before baking.

9. Bake thick sticks for 20 minutes and thin sticks for 15 minutes.

10. Immediately remove breadsticks from baking sheets and cool on a rack.

Bits & Pieces

True Italian breadsticks are crisp on the outside and chewy on the inside. Some people, however, prefer them crisp all the way through. If this is your preference, reduce the oven heat to 200 degrees and leave the baked breadsticks in the oven for one hour. Immediately remove from baking sheets and cool on a rack.

Millet Skillet Bread

Makes 12 Flat Breads

This flat bread is baked in a cast iron skillet or on a good baking stone, but can be baked on the floor of the oven. If you use the floor of your oven, remove the racks before you begin to give you plenty of room to work and so you don't burn yourself. Make sure the oven is clean! This bread is a good accompaniment to soups and stews.

1 scant tablespoon or 1 (¼-ounce) package active dry yeast
1 cup warm water (about 110 degrees)
2 tablespoons vegetable oil
1 teaspoon salt
2 teaspoons sugar
¼ cup millet
2½ to 3½ cups unbleached flour

1. In a large bowl, stir yeast into water to soften. Add oil, salt, sugar, millet, and 1 cup flour. Beat vigorously for two minutes.

2. Gradually add flour, ¼ cup at a time, until the dough begins to pull away from the side of the bowl.

3. Turn dough out onto a floured work surface. Knead, adding flour a little at a time, until you have a smooth, elastic dough.

4. Cover with a tightly woven towel and let rest on work surface for 20 minutes.

5. Preheat a cast iron skillet in the oven for 10 minutes, or a baking stone for 30 minutes, at 450 degrees. If using the floor of your oven, preheat for 10 minutes.

6. Lightly oil work surface. Divide dough into 12 balls. Flatten each ball into a 6-inch circle about one-fourth of an inch

thick. Cover with a tightly woven towel on the work surface and let rest for 10 minutes.

7. Lift the dough with a spatula and quickly drop it into the skillet, onto the stone or stove bottom. Repeat with remaining pieces. Bake 5 minutes or until lightly browned and slightly puffed. Immediately remove from the oven and wrap in a towel to cool.

Bits & Pieces

Bay leaves stored in flour containers discourage bugs.

Oriental Flat Bread

Makes 16 Flat Breads

A cooking school once asked me to teach a class on flat breads. When their brochure arrived they listed that I would teach how to make an Oriental Flat Bread. At the time, I'd never heard of one nor could I find any such bread in my library of cookbooks. In a panic, I made up this recipe. It has become one of our favorite breads...

1 scant tablespoon or 1 (¼-ounce) package active dry yeast
1¼ cups warm water (about 110 degrees)
½ teaspoon granulated sugar
½ cup chopped chives
¼ cup toasted sesame seeds*
1 cup rice flour**
2 tablespoons sesame oil
1½ to 2½ cups unbleached flour

1. In a large bowl, stir yeast into water to soften. Add sugar, chives, sesame seeds, rice flour, sesame oil, and 1 cup unbleached flour. Beat vigorously for two minutes.

2. Gradually add flour, ¼ cup at a time, until the dough begins to pull away from the side of the bowl.

3. Turn dough out onto a floured work surface. Knead, adding flour a little at a time, until you have a smooth, elastic dough.

4. Cover with a tightly woven towel and let rest on work surface for 20 minutes.

5. Lightly oil work surface. Divide dough into 16 balls. Flatten each ball into a 6-inch circle about one-fourth of an inch thick. The thickness is important, not the diameter. Place on pieces of buttered waxed or parchment paper. Cover with a tightly woven towel and let rise for 30 minutes.

6. Lift dough rounds with the paper and place on a medium-hot well-seasoned griddle or skillet with the paper side up. Gently peel off the paper and discard. Cook about 3 minutes per side, until dry and slightly browned. They should be soft and light in color.

7. Immediately remove from the skillet and wrap in a towel to cool.

*See page 61 for instructions to toast sesame seeds.
**Available in health food stores.

Bits & Pieces

Yeast doughs can be punched down and allowed to double in size at least five times before they "get tired." With each punching, the texture becomes finer and the flavor stronger.

Indian Fry Bread

Makes 16 Pieces

I usually shy away from fried foods with the exception of just a few. Once a year I love doughnuts and a couple of times a year I love this fried bread. The dough is delightfully puffy and the spicy coating of the seasoned flour gives a pleasant bite.

1 cup warm water (about 110 degrees)
1 scant tablespoon or 1 ($\frac{1}{4}$-ounce) package active dry yeast
1 teaspoon salt
1 tablespoon fresh chopped parsley or 1 teaspoon dried parsley
$3\frac{1}{2}$ cups unbleached flour, **divided**
1 tablespoon ground black pepper
1 tablespoon garlic salt
$\frac{1}{4}$ teaspoon cayenne pepper
2 cups vegetable oil for frying
Warm honey (optional)

1. In a large bowl, stir yeast into water to soften. Add salt, parsley, and 2 cups flour. Beat vigorously for two minutes.

2. Add another cup of flour, $\frac{1}{4}$ cup at a time beating well after each addition, until you have added a total of *3 cups of flour*. Dough will be soft and sticky at this point. Cover with a tightly woven towel and let rise until doubled, about one hour.

3. Combine **remaining $\frac{1}{2}$ cup of flour,** black pepper, garlic salt, and cayenne pepper. Sprinkle about half of this mixture onto the work surface. Turn dough out onto seasoned flour. Divide into 16 balls. Cover with a tightly woven towel and let rest for five minutes on the work surface.

4. Using the seasoned flour to keep dough from sticking, flatten each ball with a rolling pin until the disk of dough is about six inches in diameter and between $\frac{1}{4}$ to $\frac{1}{2}$ inch thick. Poke or cut a $\frac{1}{2}$-inch hole in the center of the dough. Many old recipes state the purpose of the hole is to "let the evil spirits out."

5. In a heavy 10-inch skillet, heat the oil to 375 degrees. Carefully place a piece of dough in the oil and let it float freely. Cook approximately 30 seconds per side. Remove from oil and drain on paper towels. Continue with the remaining dough.

6. Serve hot with warm honey.

Pita Bread

Makes 20 Pocket Breads

Pita bread is a staple of the Middle East. It goes by different names in various countries - Peda, Pide, Pitta, Ramadan Bread. It is a flat bread that puffs up when baked on the bottom of a hot oven. The hollow inside is perfect to fill with stir-fried or grilled foods. You can also use pita to shovel food from the plate to your mouth!

1 scant tablespoon or 1 (¼-ounce) package active dry yeast
1½ cups warm water (about 110 degrees)
2 teaspoons salt
3 to 4 cups unbleached flour

1.	In a large bowl, stir yeast into water to soften. Add salt and 2 cups flour. Beat vigorously for two minutes.

2.	Gradually add flour, ¼ cup at a time, until the dough begins to pull away from the side of the bowl.

3.	Turn dough out onto a floured work surface. Knead, adding flour a little at a time, until you have a smooth, elastic dough.

4.	Put dough into an oiled bowl. Turn to coat the entire ball of dough with oil. Cover with a tightly woven towel and let rise until doubled, about one hour.

5.	Turn dough out onto a lightly oiled work surface. Divide into 20 equal pieces. Shape each piece into a ball. Cover with a tightly woven towel and let rest on work surface for 10 minutes.

6.	With a rolling pin, roll each ball into a 6-inch circle. Place the circle on 6-inch squares of buttered parchment paper (parchment paper makes getting the breads from the rising surface to the oven easier).

7. Cover dough with a tightly woven towel and let rise 30 minutes.

8. About 10 minutes before baking, preheat the oven to 500 degrees. If you have a baking stone, preheat 30 minutes before baking.

9. Pita bread is best baked on a preheated baking stone placed on the lowest shelf in the oven. If you do not have a stone, preheat a heavy-duty, non-stick baking sheet in the oven for 5 minutes. The floor of the oven can be used, but is an awkward place to work and may result in burns either to you or the bread.

10. Lift dough rounds by parchment paper and flip over onto the stone or baking sheet. Peel off paper. Place 4 or 5 rounds of dough in the oven at a time. Bake 5 minutes. They should be puffy, pale in color, and flexible.

11. Immediately remove from the oven and wrap in a towel to cool. Press the air out of the pita while it is still warm.

NOTE: PITA BREAD IS BEST EATEN FRESH. THEY CAN BE TORN IN HALF TO FILL, BUT I FIND IT EASIER TO CUT THEM WITH SCISSORS. TO STORE, WRAP IN PLASTIC WRAP THEN PLACE IN A PLASTIC BAG IN THE FREEZER. THAW AND REHEAT IN A 350-DEGREE OVEN, WRAPPED IN FOIL FOR 10 MINUTES.

Variations:

*   **Whole Wheat Pitas:** Substitute 1 cup of whole wheat pastry flour for 1 cup of the unbleached flour.

*   **Parmesan Pitas:** Add 1 cup finely shredded Parmesan cheese in step 2.

*   **Sesame or Poppy Pitas:** Sprinkle the work surface lightly with the seeds of your choice before rolling out each pita. The seeds will imbed in the dough.

Pizza

Makes 4 12-inch crusts

Everyone loves pizza! I prefer to pre-bake my crust so that the crust is crisp and the cheese, which is added later, stays soft and stringy. I used to eat at a Greek restaurant in Decatur, Georgia, when I visited my parents. They served one of the best Greek pizzas I have ever tasted. I tried in vain to get the recipe and when I couldn't, I made up one. My version is every bit as good as theirs!

1 recipe of pizza dough (listed below)
1 recipe of pizza sauce (listed below)
6 cups shredded Mozzarella cheese
Topping of your choice (listed below) (optional)

1. Spread pizza dough with a thin layer of sauce.

2. Sprinkle each pizza with 1¼ cups cheese.

3. Liberally spread one or more of the toppings listed below.

Pizza Dough

1 scant tablespoon or 1 (¼-ounce) package active dry yeast
2 cups warm water (about 110 degrees)
2 tablespoons olive oil
1 teaspoon salt
5 to 6 cups unbleached flour
Cornmeal (optional)

1. In a large bowl, stir yeast into water to soften. Add olive oil, salt, and 2 cups flour. Beat vigorously for two minutes.

2. Gradually add flour, ¼ cup at a time, until the dough begins to pull away from the side of the bowl.

3. Turn dough out onto a floured work surface. Knead, adding flour a little at a time, until you have a smooth, elastic dough.

4. Put dough into an oiled bowl. Turn to coat the entire ball of dough with oil. Cover with a tightly woven towel and let rise until doubled, about one hour.

5. **WHILE THE DOUGH IS RISING, PREPARE THE SAUCE** (See next page).

6. Turn dough out onto a lightly oiled work surface and divide into 4 pieces. Using the heel of your hand, flatten each piece of dough into a 12-inch round, or if you're feeling adventuresome, you can toss the dough into the air with a spinning motion until the dough is about 12 inches in diameter (be prepared for some good laughs!). Place onto a well-greased 12-inch pizza pan. For a crispier crust, sprinkle the pan with cornmeal before adding the dough. Press around the edge of the dough to make a slight rise or lip to keep the sauce and topping from spilling over. Cover with a tightly woven towel and let rise for 20 minutes.

7. About 10 minutes before baking, preheat oven to 400 degrees.

8. Prick the dough every 3 inches with the tines of a fork to prevent large bubbles from developing in the dough.

9. Bake for 10 minutes or until the crust is firm, but flexible.

10. Immediately remove bread from pans and cool on a rack, OR immediately spread with sauce, sprinkle with cheese, and add toppings from the list below (optional) then return to the oven for 10 minutes or until the edges are lightly browned.

Pizza Sauce

1 cup finely chopped onions
4 cloves finely chopped garlic
4 tablespoons olive oil
3 1-pound cans chopped tomatoes
3 tablespoons chopped fresh basil or 1 tablespoon dried basil
3 tablespoons chopped fresh oregano or 1 tablespoon dried
　oregano
1 teaspoon granulated sugar
1 teaspoon salt
½ teaspoon cracked pepper
1 6-ounce can tomato paste

1.　Sauté onions and garlic in olive oil. Add tomatoes, basil,
　　oregano, sugar, salt, cracked pepper, and tomato paste and
　　stir to combine. Bring mixture to a boil, reduce heat, and
　　simmer for one hour, stirring occasionally to keep the sauce
　　from sticking. Allow mixture to cool.

Optional toppings:

Sautéed Italian sausage, crumbled
Black and/or green olives, quartered or sliced
Sautéed ground beef, crumbled
Crisply fried bacon, crumbled
Canadian bacon, thinly sliced
Anchovies
Artichoke hearts, cut into slivers
Salami, thinly sliced
Mushrooms, sliced
Chopped ham and pineapple chunks
Pepperoni, thinly sliced
Bell peppers, thinly sliced
Onion rings
Blanched vegetables, thinly sliced

Variation:

- **Greek Pizza:** Spread crust with a thin layer of pizza sauce. Top with 2 cups shredded mozzarella cheese, 1 cup *each* sautéed thinly sliced green peppers and onions, ½ cup pitted Greek olive halves, and ½ cup crumbled Feta cheese. Bake 5 minutes longer than a regular pizza.

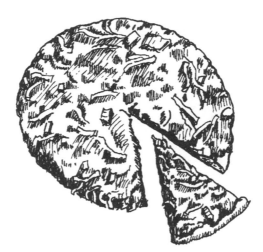

Tomato Cheese Batter Bread

Serves 6-8

This tasty tomato-cheese bread is quick and easy. Batter breads are beaten and not kneaded. The consistency is somewhere between biscuits and a yeast loaf. Batter breads only rise once which means you can have it on the table in less than two hours (even less time if you use one of the quick-rising yeasts).

2 tablespoons butter
2 cups unbleached flour
1 tablespoon sugar
½ teaspoon salt
1 scant tablespoon or 1 (¼-ounce) package active dry yeast
¼ cup soft butter
1 cup crushed tomatoes in juice
1 egg, beaten
¾ cup Parmesan cheese, shredded
2 tablespoons fresh parsley, chopped

1. Cut 2 tablespoons butter into ¼-inch dice. Place on a piece of waxed paper and put in the freezer.

2. In a large bowl, combine flour, sugar, salt, and yeast.

3. Heat soft butter and tomatoes to 125 degrees. Add to the dry ingredients with the egg, Parmesan cheese, and parsley. Beat vigorously for two minutes.

4. Turn dough into a well-greased, 8-inch round pan. Cover with a tightly woven towel and let rise for one hour.

5. About 10 minutes before baking, preheat oven to 375 degree.

6. Just before baking, remove the diced butter from the freezer and sprinkle on the top of the dough.

7. Bake for 20 minutes, or until the internal temperature of the bread beaches 190 degrees.

8. Serve immediately cut in pie-shaped wedges.

Bits & Pieces

Breads containing eggs tend to brown quicker than other breads. Watch your bread the last ten minutes of baking. You may need to cover it with foil to keep it from getting too dark.

Veggie & Sausage Calzone

Makes 12 Calzones

Calzone (pronounced cal-zone-ay) is a disk of dough folded around a variety of fillings. Some contain a combination of herbs and vegetables, while others have meat. Get creative and develop a calzone with your favorite filling.

1 scant tablespoon or 1 (¼-ounce) package active dry yeast
½ cup warm water (about 110 degrees)
1 tablespoon granulated sugar
1 teaspoon salt
2½ 3½ cups unbleached flour
½ pound spicy Italian sausage
1 cup thinly sliced bell peppers
1 cup thinly sliced onions
5 tablespoons olive oil, *divided*
1 tablespoon finely minced garlic, *divided*
1 cup thinly sliced carrots
1 cup thinly sliced broccoli
2 cups shredded provolone cheese (about 8 ounces)
1 tablespoon fresh oregano leaves or 1 teaspoon dried oregano
    leaves
1 tablespoon fresh basil leaves or 1 teaspoon dried basil leaves
Salt and pepper to taste

1. In a large bowl, stir the yeast into water to soften. Add sugar, salt, and 2 cups flour. Beat vigorously for two minutes.

2. Gradually add flour, ¼ cup at a time, until the dough begins to pull away from the side of the bowl.

3. Turn dough out onto a floured work surface. Knead, adding flour a little at a time, until you have a smooth, elastic dough.

4. Put dough into an oiled bowl. Turn to coat the entire ball of dough with oil. Cover with a tightly woven towel and let rise until doubled, about one hour.

5. **WHILE DOUGH RISES, PREPARE STEPS 6 THROUGH 9.**

6. Remove sausage from casing and brown over medium heat. Break sausage into small chunks while cooking. Drain. Set aside to cool.

7. In a large skillet, over medium-low heat, combine peppers, onion, and *2 tablespoons olive oil.* Cook, stirring often until onions and peppers are limp, about 30 minutes. Add *1 teaspoon of garlic* and cook for two more minutes. Set aside to cool.

8. Bring a pot of water to a full boil. Add the carrots and cook for 2 minutes. Place broccoli in a strainer over the sink. Pour carrots and water over the broccoli. Drain. Set aside to cool.

9. Combine *the remaining garlic* with the *remaining olive oil* over low heat. Simmer for 15 minutes. Remove from heat and set aside to cool.

10. Turn the dough out onto a lightly oiled work surface and divide into 12 pieces. Shape each piece into a ball. Cover with a tightly woven towel and let rest on work surface for 5 minutes.

11. Combine sausage, onion mixture, carrots and broccoli, cheese, oregano, basil, salt, and pepper. Divide filling into 12 equal portions.

12. With a rolling pin, roll each ball of dough into a 6-inch circle. Place a portion of the filling mixture in the center of each circle. Fold the circle in half and press the edges to seal. Place on two parchment-lined baking sheets (six on each pan). Cover with a tightly woven towel and let rise for 25 minutes.

13. About 10 minutes before baking, preheat oven to 400 degrees. Place a shallow pan on the bottom shelf of the oven.

14. Just before baking, crimp the edges of each calzone with a fork. This helps keep the filling inside where it belongs. Brush each calzone with the *garlic-oil mixture*. Prick the top with a fork in two or three places. This allows the air to escape so the calzone doesn't puff up like a balloon.

15. Place 5 ice cubes in the hot pan on the bottom shelf. Immediately put the calzone into oven. Close the door quickly to prevent steam from escaping and bake for 25 minutes, or until golden brown.

16. Immediately remove calzone from baking sheets and place on a rack. Brush once again with the *garlic-oil mixture*.

NOTE: BEST SERVED WARM. STORE COOLED, LEFTOVER CALZONE IN A PLASTIC ZIP-STYLE BAG IN THE REFRIGERATOR FOR UP TO THREE DAYS. REHEAT ON A BAKING SHEET IN A 375 DEGREE OVEN FOR 10 MINUTES.

Bits & Pieces

How do you pronounce calzone – cal-zōne, cal-zōn-ee, cal-zōne-ay? Most Americans pronounce it "cal-zōn-ee" however, in Italy it is pronounced with a long "a" at the end – cal-zōne-ay. No matter how you pronounce it, you'll probably be understood and get what you want.

Sweet Breads

Bavarian Nussstollen

This showy nut bread comes from Bavaria in Southern Germany. The subtle spices complement the ground nuts. This bread is good at room temperature, but warming it brings out the flavors even more. By the way, Nussstollen really does have three "S's"!

2 scant tablespoons or 2 (¼-ounce) packages active dry yeast
½ cup warm water (about 110 degrees)
1½ cups warm milk (about 110 degrees)
½ cup soft butter
½ cup granulated sugar
2 teaspoons salt
3 large eggs, separated
2 teaspoons pure vanilla extract
2 teaspoons grated lemon peel
½ teaspoon ground cardamom
½ teaspoon ground ginger
½ teaspoon ground mace
5½ to 6½ cups unbleached flour
2 cups ground hazelnuts
½ cup firmly packed brown sugar
2 teaspoons cinnamon
2 cups powdered sugar
7 to 9 tablespoons heavy cream

1. In a large bowl, stir yeast into water to soften. Add milk, butter, granulated sugar, salt, egg yolks, vanilla, lemon peel, cardamom, ginger, mace, and 3 cups flour. Beat vigorously for two minutes.

2. Gradually add flour, ¼ cup at a time, until the dough begins to pull away from the side of the bowl.

3. Turn dough out onto a floured work surface. Knead, adding flour a little at a time, until you have a smooth, elastic dough.

4. Put dough into an oiled bowl. Turn to coat the entire ball of dough with oil. Cover with a tightly woven towel and let rise until doubled, about one hour.

5. Beat egg whites until stiff peaks form. Set aside.

6. Combine hazelnuts, brown sugar, and cinnamon. Gently fold in egg whites.

7. Turn dough out onto a lightly oiled work surface and divide in half. With a rolling pin, roll each half of the dough into a 12 by 20-inch rectangle. Spread half the hazelnut mixture on each rectangle. Roll up into a 20-inch cylinder. Place cylinders on a parchment-lined baking sheet. Cut the dough in half lengthwise. Separate the dough, exposing the inside of the cylinder. At each end, cross the halves (with the inner layers facing up) forming a twist. Pinch ends together. Cover and let rise until doubled, about 45 minutes.

8. About 10 minutes before baking, preheat oven to 375 degrees.

9. Bake for 25 minutes, or until the internal temperature of the loaf reaches 190 degrees.

10. Immediately remove bread from baking sheet and cool on a rack for 20 minutes.

11. Combine powdered sugar and cream. Mixture should be the consistency of honey (if it isn't, adjust by adding more cream to thin it or powdered sugar to thicken it). Drizzle over the top of each nussstollen.

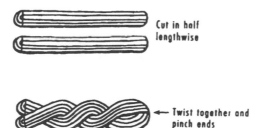

Cut in half
lengthwise

Twist together and
pinch ends

Braided Fruit Wreath

Makes 2 Wreaths

Though this recipe makes two wreaths, you can shape the dough into one large showy one by working with three strands of dough in step 5 – a magnificent edible centerpiece for the holidays.

2 scant tablespoons or 2 (¼-ounce) packages active dry yeast
½ cup warm water (about 110 degrees)
1 cup warm milk (about 110 degrees)
½ cup soft butter
½ cup granulated sugar
½ teaspoon mace
2 tablespoons grated lemon rind
2 large eggs, beaten
2 teaspoons salt
4½ to 5½ cups unbleached flour
1 cup finely chopped hazelnuts
2 cups diced mixed candied fruits
2 cups powdered sugar
7 to 9 tablespoons heavy cream

1.	In a large bowl, stir yeast into water to soften. Add milk, butter, sugar, mace, lemon rind, eggs, salt, and 2 cups flour. Beat vigorously for two minutes.

2.	Gradually add flour, ¼ cup at a time, until the dough begins to pull away from the side of the bowl.

3.	Turn dough out onto a floured work surface. Knead, adding flour a little at a time, until you have a smooth, elastic dough.

4.	Put dough into an oiled bowl. Turn to coat the entire ball of dough with oil. Cover with a tightly woven towel and let rise until doubled, about one hour.

5.	Turn dough out onto a lightly oiled work surface and divide in half. Using a rolling pin, roll half of the dough into a

22 by 9-inch rectangle. Cover and let rest 5 minutes on the work surface.

6. Cut the dough into three 22-inch long strips.

7. Mix the nuts and candied fruit. Fill the center of each strip with ½ cup of the nut and fruit mixture. Bring edges together and pinch to seal forming three 22-inch-long strands.

8. Lay the strands side-by-side on a parchment-lined baking sheet. Turn the baking sheet so the strands are facing lengthwise away from you. Starting in the center of the strands, place the right strand over the middle strand (the right strand has now become the middle strand), then the left strand over the middle, the right over the middle, left over the middle, etc. Continue this process until the strands are too short to braid. Do not pinch the ends together.

9. To braid the other end of the loaf, turn the baking sheet around so that the unbraided portion is facing you. Place the middle strand over the right strand, then middle strand over the left, middle over the right, middle over the left, etc., until the ends are too short to braid. Join the ends of the braid to form a wreath, and pinch to seal. Repeat with other half of the dough. Cover with a tightly woven towel and let rise until almost doubled, about 45 minutes.

10. About 10 minutes before baking, preheat oven to 375 degrees.

11. Bake for 25 minutes, or until the internal temperature of the loaf reaches 190 degrees.

12. Immediately remove bread from baking sheet and cool on a rack for 20 minutes.

13. Combine powdered sugar and cream. Mixture should be the consistency of honey (if it isn't, adjust by adding more cream to thin it or powdered sugar to thicken it). Drizzle over the top of each wreath.

Cynthia's Spudnuts

Makes about 5 Dozen

I received this recipe from my friend Cynthia Webb when we lived in Norfolk, VA. My mouth waters when I think about her Spudnuts. They remind me of good old Krispy Kreme doughnuts from the South - so light they melt in your mouth!

2 scant tablespoons or 2 (¼-ounce) packages active dry yeast
½ cup warm water (about 110 degrees)
1 cup warm mashed potatoes (about 110 degrees)(See "Bits & Pieces" on next page)
6 tablespoons vegetable shortening
2 teaspoons vanilla extract, *divided*
1½ cups warm milk (about 110 degrees)
2 large eggs, separated
5 cups unbleached flour
1 teaspoon salt
2 tablespoons granulated sugar
Oil for frying
1 pound powdered sugar
8 to 10 tablespoons cold milk

1. In a large bowl, stir yeast into water to soften. Add potatoes, shortening, *1½ teaspoons vanilla,* warm milk, and egg yolks. Beat mixture until well blended.

2. Beat the egg whites until stiff peaks form. Fold into the yeast mixture.

3. Combine flour, salt, and sugar and stir into the yeast mixture. Cover with a tightly woven towel and let rise for 1 hour. Mixture will be very soft.

4. Turn dough out onto a heavily floured board and roll with a rolling pin to ¼-inch thick. Cut with a doughnut cutter, cover with a tightly woven towel and let rise for 30 minutes.

Brush excess flour from dough scraps and knead into a ball. Cover with a tightly woven towel and let dough rest for 5 minutes before re-rolling.

5. In a deep pan (at least four inches deep), heat two inches of oil to 375 degrees – for safety's sake, you should have about two inches of space between the oil and the top of the pan.

6. Carefully drop three or four spudnuts, one at a time, into the oil. *Do not crowd.* Fry two minutes on each side until lightly browned. Remove with a slotted spoon and drain on paper towels. Glaze while warm.

7. For the glaze, combine powdered sugar, *remaining vanilla,* and milk. The mixture should be thinner than honey – more like syrup. Pour into a flat bowl – such as a cereal bowl. Dip both sides of the spudnuts into the mixture. Drain on a rack. Excess glaze can be scraped back into the bowl and reused.

Bits & Pieces

To mash potatoes, place unpeeled potatoes in a saucepan and cover with water. Cover the saucepan and bring water to a boil. Cook potatoes until tender (about 25 minutes depending on the size of your potatoes). They'll be soft when you stick a knife blade into their center. Drain water from the pan into a container (use this water to make bread, don't throw it out). Let potatoes sit until cool enough to peel. Cut potatoes into chunks, mash, either by hand with a potato masher or in a food processor or mixer, until no lumps remain. You can use instant mashed potatoes in bread recipes, but don't add salt when preparing them. Make sure the potatoes have cooled to about 110 degrees before adding to any yeast mixture.

German Butterkuchen

Makes 12 3-Inch Squares

This buttery batter bread is beaten rather than kneaded. It rises in the refrigerator overnight which makes it a great coffeecake to have for breakfast without having to get up at the crack of dawn to prepare it.

1 scant tablespoon or 1 (¼-ounce) package active dry yeast
½ cup warm water (about 110 degrees)
1¼ cups warm milk (about 110 degrees)
½ cup soft butter
2 large eggs, beaten
1 teaspoon salt
½ cup granulated sugar
4 cups unbleached flour
1 cup firmly packed brown sugar
1½ teaspoons ground cinnamon
½ cup very cold butter
½ cup coarsely chopped walnuts

1. In a large bowl, stir yeast into water to soften. Add milk, soft butter, eggs, salt, granulated sugar, and flour. Beat vigorously for two minutes.

2. Spread dough evenly into a well-greased 9 by 13-inch baking pan.

3. With a whisk combine brown sugar and cinnamon. Cut in cold butter until the butter is about the size of rice kernels. Add walnuts and toss to combine. Sprinkle evenly over batter.

4. Lightly lay a piece of plastic wrap over the topping then cover with a tightly woven towel. Refrigerate 8 to 24 hours.

5. About 10 minutes before baking, preheat oven to 375 degrees (350 degrees if using a glass pan).

6. Bake for 25 minutes, or until the internal temperature of the loaf reaches 190 degrees.

7. Let Kuchen sit for 15 minutes in pan before cutting in squares and serving.

Bits & Pieces

Glass pans conduct heat differently than metal pans. Unless specifically stated to use a glass pan, oven temperatures are set for metal pans. If you use a glass (Pyrex-type) pan, always reduce the oven temperature 25 degrees.

Greek Easter Twist

For Easter, many Greeks dye eggs a bright red to symbolize the blood of Christ. They have a charming game for cracking the eggs that is played by both the young and old. Two people each take an egg and, holding them by the large end, take turns trying to crack the other's egg by striking it with their own. The person whose egg cracks first loses. The winner has good luck all year long.

2 scant tablespoons or 2 (¼-ounce) packages active dry yeast
½ cup warm water (about 110 degrees)
1 cup warm milk (about 110 degrees)
1 cup soft butter
4 large eggs, beaten
½ cup honey
1 tablespoon crushed anise seed
1 tablespoon grated orange peel
2 teaspoons salt
6 to 7 cups unbleached flour
8 to 12 hard-boiled eggs, dyed bright red
Glaze - 1 egg beaten with 1 tablespoon of water
Coarse sugar or sesame seeds

1. In a large bowl, stir yeast into water to soften. Add milk, butter, eggs, honey, anise seed, orange peel, salt, and 3 cups flour. Beat vigorously for two minutes.

2. Gradually add flour, ¼ cup at a time, until the dough begins to pull away from the side of the bowl.

3. Turn dough out onto a floured work surface. Knead, adding flour a little at a time, until you have a smooth, elastic dough.

4. Put dough into an oiled bowl. Turn to coat the entire ball of dough with oil. Cover with a tightly woven towel and let rise until doubled, about one hour.

5. Turn the dough out onto a lightly oiled work surface and divide in fourths. Shape each fourth into a 30-inch strand. Twist two strands together and join the ends. Spread dough and insert four to six eggs evenly spaced between the strands. Place onto parchment-lined baking sheets. Repeat with the remaining two strands. Cover with a tightly woven towel and let rise until almost doubled, about 45 minutes.

6. About 10 minutes before baking, preheat oven to 375 degrees.

7. Just before baking, brush each loaf lightly with the glaze and sprinkle with the coarse sugar or seeds.

8. Bake for 25 minutes, or until the internal temperature of the loaf reaches 190 degrees.

9. Immediately remove bread from baking sheets and cool on a rack.

Gugelhopf

This marvelous batter bread comes from Austria. The Austrians allegedly designed the special Gugelhopf pan in the style of a turban to mock the Turks who tried to rule them. The bread is delightfully rich and tastes wonderful fresh from the oven. The leftovers (if there are any) are great lightly buttered then toasted.

1 scant tablespoon or 1 (¼-ounce) package active dry yeast
¼ cup warm water (about 110 degrees)
½ cup warm milk (about 110 degrees)
½ cup soft butter
12 egg yolks
1 teaspoon salt
½ cup granulated sugar
¼ teaspoon almond extract
2 teaspoons lemon rind
4 cups unbleached flour
½ cup golden raisins
½ cup slivered almonds
½ cup ground almonds
Powdered sugar (optional)

1. In a large bowl, stir yeast into water to soften. Add milk, butter, yolks, salt, sugar, almond extract, lemon rind, and 1 cup flour. Beat vigorously for two minutes.

2. Gradually add the remaining flour, ¼ cup at a time, beating well after each addition. Gugelhopf is beaten rather than kneaded. Once all of the flour has been added, beat for three minutes. Cover with plastic wrap and let rise until doubled, about 1½ hours.

3. Stir the dough down, and add the raisins and slivered almonds.

4. Heavily butter a Gugelhopf mold (a bundt or tube pan can be substituted). Sprinkle the bottom and sides of the mold with ground almonds. Spoon the dough into the mold, cover with plastic wrap, and let rise until almost doubled, about 1 hour.

5. About 10 minutes before baking, preheat the oven to 350 degrees.

6. Bake for 45 minutes or until the internal temperature of the bread reaches 190 degrees. Watch the bread carefully during the last 10 minutes of baking so that it does not get too brown. If it does brown too much, cover the mold with foil (with the shiny side facing away from the loaf) to prevent any more browning.

7. Immediately remove bread from the pan and cool on a rack.

8. Just before serving, sprinkle loaf liberally with powdered sugar.

Mincemeat Orange Rolls

Makes 24 Rolls

Most people seem to think of mincemeat as a holiday ingredient. These tasty rolls are great any time of the year, but are especially good for a holiday brunch or breakfast. The pungent sweet and sour flavor of mincemeat is perfect in this lightly sweetened bread dough. The rolls are shaped like cinnamon rolls and are easy to form into a Christmas tree if you want a festive presentation.

2 scant tablespoons or 2 (¼-ounce) packages active dry yeast
½ cup warm water (about 110 degrees)
2 cups warm milk (about 110 degrees)
1 teaspoon vanilla extract
2 large eggs, beaten
¼ cup soft butter
¼ cup granulated sugar
2 teaspoons salt
2 tablespoons grated fresh orange peel
6 to 7 cups unbleached flour
2 cups finely chopped mincemeat (homemade or store-bought)
1½ cups powdered sugar
3 to 5 tablespoons orange juice

1. In a large bowl, stir yeast into water to soften. Add milk, vanilla, eggs, butter, sugar, salt, orange peel and 2 cups flour. Beat vigorously for two minutes.

2. Gradually add flour, ¼ cup at a time, until the dough begins to pull away from the side of the bowl.

3. Turn dough out onto a floured work surface. Knead, adding flour a little at a time, until you have a smooth, elastic dough.

4. Put dough into an oiled bowl. Turn to coat the entire ball of dough with oil. Cover with a tightly woven towel and let rise until doubled, about one hour.

5. Turn the dough out onto a lightly oiled work surface and divide in half. Roll each half with a rolling pin into a 15 by 18-inch rectangle. Spread each half with mincemeat, leaving a ½-inch strip along one of the long edges free. Roll up into a 15-inch cylinder. Pinch the loose edge to the cylinder. Cut each cylinder into 12 slices* (for easy cutting, see "Bits & Pieces" below). Place rolls with the cut side up in two parchment-lined or well-greased 9 by 13 by 2-inch baking pans. Cover with a tightly woven towel and let rise until almost doubled, about 45 minutes.

6. About 10 minutes before baking, preheat oven to 375 degrees (350 degrees if using glass pans – See "Bits & Pieces" on page 161).

7. Bake for 20 minutes, or until the internal temperature of the rolls reaches 190 degrees.

8. Immediately remove rolls from pans and cool on a rack for 15 minutes.

9. Combine powdered sugar with enough orange juice to make a spreadable icing. Spread on top of warm rolls.

*To make a holiday tree, roll the dough with a rolling pin into an 18-inch cylinder and cut into 16 pieces. Put cut rolls in a triangle on your baking sheet (one on the first row, two on the second, three on the third, etc.) to form a tree, then one centered on the last row to form the trunk of the tree.

Bits & Pieces

The best way to cut cinnamon rolls so they keep their shape is with a 14-inch strand of plain, unwaxed dental floss. Wrap the floss around each of your index fingers and pull taut. Lightly score the top of the cylinder with the floss so you'll know where to cut. Slip the floss under the roll where you scored it, bring up the ends of the floss, cross them, and pull straight out to the sides.

Panettone

This recipe was given to me in Dallas by a 90-year old lady in our church. It had been used in her family for many years. I have altered it slightly to be more specific in the measurements. Candied fruits, citron, and candied fruit peels are available in grocery stores from November through the holiday season. You may have trouble finding them after that time, but they have a very long shelf life so you can stock up if you wish to use them throughout the year.

1 scant tablespoon or 1 (¼-ounce) package active dry yeast
¼ cup warm water (about 110 degrees)
1½ cups warm milk (about 110 degrees)
½ cup granulated sugar
1 teaspoon salt
¼ cup soft butter
4½ to 5½ cups unbleached flour
2 teaspoons anise seeds
¾ cup golden raisins
½ cup pine nuts
½ cup pistachio nuts
½ cup candied lemon peel
¼ cup candied citron
2 tablespoons grated fresh orange peel

1. In a large bowl, stir yeast into water to soften. Add milk, sugar, salt, butter, and 1 cup flour. Beat vigorously for two minutes.

2. With a mortar and pestle, crush the anise seeds. Combine crushed seeds, raisins, pine nuts, pistachio nuts, lemon peel, citron, and orange peel and mix well. Add to the yeast mixture. Beat vigorously for two minutes.

3.   Gradually add flour, ¼ cup at a time, until the dough begins to pull away from the side of the bowl.

4.   Turn dough out onto a floured work surface. Knead, adding flour a little at a time, until you have a smooth, elastic dough.

5.   Put dough into an oiled bowl. Turn to coat the entire ball of dough with oil. Cover with a tightly woven towel and let rise until doubled, about one hour.

6.   Turn dough out onto a lightly oiled work surface and shape into a ball. Let rest 5 minutes.

7.   Put dough into a well-greased Panettone pan. You can also punch a large hole in the center of the dough and slip over the center post of a well-greased bundt or tube pan. Cover with a tightly woven towel and let rise until almost doubled, about one hour.

8.   About 10 minutes before baking, preheat oven to 375 degrees.

9.   Bake for 45 minutes, or until the internal temperature of the loaf reaches 190 degrees.

10.   Immediately remove bread from pan and cool on a rack.

Bits & Pieces

A mortar is a bowl-shaped utensil and a pestle is a fat, round-ended stick. The pestle is used to grind spices, herbs, and seeds in the mortar to release the flavors. It is also used to turn oily foods into a paste.

Scandinavian Coffee Braid

Makes 2 Braids

This attractive, bittersweet braid is basted with a strong coffee mixture that produces a lovely dark crust. It is then sprinkled with bright-white, coarse sugar. The cardamom and nuts add an intriguing taste and texture.

2 scant tablespoons or 2 (¼-ounce) packages active dry yeast
½ cup warm water (about 110 degrees)
1½ cups warm milk (about 110 degrees)
½ cup soft butter
½ cup firmly packed dark brown sugar
2 teaspoons salt
2 tablespoons instant coffee
4 large eggs, beaten
2 teaspoons ground cardamom
1 cup coarsely chopped walnuts
6 to 7 cups unbleached flour
Glaze - 3 tablespoons instant coffee stirred into 4 tablespoons
   water
Parlsucker or coarse sugar*

1. In a large bowl, stir yeast into water to soften. Add milk, butter, sugar, salt, coffee, eggs, cardamom, walnuts, and 3 cups flour. Beat vigorously for two minutes.

2. Gradually add flour, ¼ cup at a time, until the dough begins to pull away from the side of the bowl.

3. Turn dough out onto a floured work surface. Knead, adding flour a little at a time, until you have a smooth, elastic dough.

4. Put dough into an oiled bowl. Turn to coat the entire ball of dough with oil. Cover with a tightly woven towel and let rise until doubled, about one hour.

5. Turn the dough out onto a lightly oiled work surface and divide in sixths. Shape each piece of dough into a 20-inch

strand. Lay three strands side-by-side on a parchment-lined baking sheet. Turn the baking sheet so the strands are facing lengthwise away from you. Starting in the center of the strands, place the right strand over the middle strand (the right strand has now become the middle strand), then the left strand over the middle, the right over the middle, left over the middle, etc. Continue this process until the strands are too short to braid. Pinch all ends together and tuck them under.

6. To braid the other end of the loaf, turn the baking sheet around so that the unbraided portion is facing you. Place the middle strand over the right strand, then the middle strand over the left, middle over the right, middle over the left, etc., until the ends are too short to braid. Pinch all three ends together and tuck them under. Repeat with the remaining three strands. Cover with a tightly woven towel and let rise until almost doubled, about 45 minutes.

7. About 10 minutes before baking, preheat oven to 375 degrees.

8. Just before baking, brush each braid with the glaze and sprinkle with the coarse sugar.

9. Bake for 25 minutes, or until the internal temperature of the loaves reaches 190 degrees.

10. Immediately remove bread from baking sheet and cool on a rack.

*Parlsucher can be purchased from the King Arthur Flour Baker's Catalogue (see "Sources" on page 183).

Bits & Pieces

I always recommend braiding loaves from the middle. If you braid from one end to the other, invariably the loaf gets thinner as you braid. If you start in the center and braid to one end, turn the loaf and braid from the center to the other end, the loaf will be plump in the center and tapered to the ends of the loaf giving a balanced shape.

Sin-Amen Rolls

These aptly-named, crisp-crusted rolls have very little liquid, but lots of butter and eggs. Their flavor bursts in your mouth enticing you to eat more, more, more! When kneading the dough, add as little flour as possible and leave the dough slightly sticky at the end of the kneading period. The rolls will turn out lighter and crispier. The Sin-Amen Rolls are best served shortly after baking.

1 scant tablespoon or 1 (¼-ounce) package active dry yeast
½ cup warm water (about 110 degrees)
1 tablespoon grated lemon peel
1 teaspoon pure vanilla
¼ cup soft butter
¼ cup granulated sugar
3 large eggs
1 teaspoon salt
½ cup raisins (optional)
3 to 3½ cups unbleached flour
¾ cup firmly packed light brown sugar
1 teaspoon cinnamon
¼ cup melted butter or canola oil

1. In a large bowl, stir yeast into water to soften. Add lemon peel, vanilla, soft butter, granulated sugar, large eggs, salt, raisins, and 2 cups flour. Beat vigorously for two minutes.

2. Gradually add flour, ¼ cup at a time, until the dough begins to pull away from the side of the bowl.

3. Turn dough out onto a floured work surface. Knead, adding flour a little at a time, until you have a smooth, elastic dough. Remember, add as little flour to this dough as possible.

4. Put dough into an oiled bowl. Turn to coat the entire ball of dough with oil. Cover with a tightly woven towel and let rise until doubled, about 1½ hours.

5. Combine brown sugar and cinnamon in a flat bowl. Pour oil into another bowl.

6. Turn the dough out onto a lightly oiled work surface and divide into 24 pieces. Shape each piece into a ball. Dip each ball into melted butter or oil, then roll in sugar-cinnamon mixture. Place balls into well-greased muffin pans. Cover with a tightly woven towel and let rise until almost doubled, about 45 minutes.

7. About 10 minutes before baking, preheat oven to 375 degrees.

8. Bake for 20 minutes, or until the internal temperature of the rolls reaches 190 degrees.

9. Immediately remove rolls from pans and serve warm.

Whole Wheat Cinnamon Rum Rolls

Makes 30 Rolls

These rolls are hearty and light. They are quite different from regular cinnamon rolls since they are made entirely with whole wheat flour. You must be careful not to add too much flour to this recipe or the rolls will come out heavy. The addition of rum to the glaze complements the wonderfully, nutty taste of the whole wheat.

2 scant tablespoons or 2 (¼-ounce) packages active dry yeast
½ cup warm water (about 110 degrees)
1½ cups warm milk (about 110 degrees)
½ cup vegetable shortening
½ cup honey
3 large eggs
1 tablespoon lemon juice
2 teaspoons salt
3 tablespoons soy flour (optional)
5½ to 6½ cups whole wheat flour
¼ cup melted butter
1 cup firmly packed brown sugar
3 tablespoons cinnamon
½ cup raisins (optional)
½ cup chopped nuts (optional)
2 cups powdered sugar
1 tablespoon rum extract
5 to 7 tablespoons heavy cream

1. In a large bowl, stir yeast into water to soften. Add milk, shortening, honey, eggs, lemon juice, salt, soy flour, and 2 cups whole wheat flour. Beat vigorously for two minutes.

2. Gradually add flour, ¼ cup at a time, until the dough begins to pull away from the side of the bowl.

3.   Turn dough out onto a floured work surface. Knead, adding flour a little at a time, until you have a smooth, elastic dough.

4.   Put dough into an oiled bowl. Turn to coat the entire ball of dough with oil. Cover with a tightly woven towel and let rise until doubled, about one hour.

5.   Turn the dough out onto a lightly oiled work surface and divide in half. Roll each half with a rolling pin into a 12 by 18-inch rectangle. Brush dough with melted butter, leaving a ½-inch border along one long side of the rectangle free of butter..

6.   Combine brown sugar, cinnamon, raisins and nuts. Sprinkle evenly over each portion of dough. Roll up into two 18-inch cylinders and pinch the loose edge to the cylinder. Cut into 30 rolls* (15 from each cylinder) and place cut-side up into two parchment-lined 9 by 13-inch pans. Cover with a tightly woven towel and let rise until almost doubled, about 45 minutes.

7.   About 10 minutes before baking, preheat oven to 375 degrees (350 degrees if using glass pans – see page 161).

8.   Bake for 20 minutes or until the internal temperature of the rolls reaches 190 degrees.

9.   Leave the rolls in the pan to cool since they benefit from the steam - it makes them softer. Allow the rolls to cool for 15 minutes.

10. Combine powdered sugar, rum extract, and milk. Mixture should be the consistency of honey (if it isn't, adjust by adding more cream to thin it or powdered sugar to thicken it). Drizzle over the top of the rolls.

*See "Bits & Pieces" on page 167 for a slick way to cut cinnamon rolls.

Cottage Cheese Stollen

Makes 4 Stollens

This is not a traditional Stollen by any means, but it is showy and extremely tasty. Since I love to give Stollens to friends and family during the holidays, I've written the recipe to yield four. It can easily be halved, and it freezes nicely. You can use either candied fruits or dried fruits. The cottage cheese in the dough keeps the bread light and moist.

2 tablespoons grated orange peel
1 tablespoon grated lemon peel
1 cup granulated sugar, *divided*
2 cups mixed candied fruits or mixed diced dried fruits
1 cup raisins
½ cup juice from orange and lemon used for peel, or ½ cup
   orange juice
1 cup cottage cheese
½ cup plain yogurt
¼ cup soft butter
1 cup boiling water
2 scant tablespoons or 2 (¼-ounce) packages active dry yeast
½ cup warm water (about 110 degrees)
1 cup slivered almonds, toasted
2 teaspoons salt
9½ to 10½ cups unbleached flour
¼ cup melted butter
¼ cup ground cinnamon
2 cups powdered sugar
7 to 9 tablespoons heavy cream

1.   Combine orange and lemon peel*, *½ cup granulated sugar*, candied fruit, raisins, and juice. Set aside.

2.   In a food processor or blender, puree cottage cheese and yogurt until smooth. If you do not have a processor or blender, press the cottage cheese through a strainer or food

mill to remove the lumps, then combine with the yogurt. Add soft butter and boiling water. Set aside.

3. In a large bowl, stir yeast into warm water to soften. Add fruit mixture, cheese mixture, almonds, salt, and 5 cups of flour. Beat vigorously for two minutes.

4. Gradually add flour, ¼ cup at a time, until the dough begins to pull away from the side of the bowl.

5. Turn dough out onto a floured work surface. Knead, adding flour a little at a time, until you have a smooth, elastic dough.

6. Put dough into an oiled bowl. Turn to coat the entire ball of dough with oil. Cover with a tightly woven towel and let rise until doubled, about two hours.

7. Turn the dough out onto a lightly oiled work surface. Divide the dough in fourths. With a rolling pin, roll each portion of dough into a 9 by 13-inch oval. Brush one tablespoon melted butter on each oval. Sprinkle *2 tablespoons granulated sugar* over one half of each oval lengthwise then sprinkle with 1 tablespoon of cinnamon. Fold dough in half lengthwise. Carefully lift stollens and place 2 per parchment-lined baking sheet. Press on the folded side slightly to help the loaf keep its shape during rising and baking. Cover with a tightly woven towel and let rise until almost doubled, about one hour.

8. About 10 minutes before baking, preheat oven to 375 degrees.

9. Bake for 25 minutes, or until the internal temperature of the loaf reaches 190 degrees.

10. Immediately remove bread from baking sheets and cool on a rack for 20 minutes.

11. Combine powdered sugar and cream. Mixture should be the consistency of honey (if it isn't, adjust by adding more

cream to thin it or powdered sugar to thicken it). Drizzle over the top of each Stollen.

Bits & Pieces

I prefer to cook all sweet breads on parchment-lined baking sheets. Not only is it easier to clean up after baking, but the parchment paper keeps dough with a high sugar content from caramelizing on the pan - this keeps the bottom of the loaves softer.

Trouble Shooting And Sources

	Too much salt	Too much sweetener	Too much flour	Flour is old	Too much yeast	Yeast is old	Yeast over-fermented	Yeast not properly activated **	May not have added salt or sugar	Dry ingredients not fully dissolved ***	Bowl greased too heavily
1. Dough doesn't rise	◉	◉	◉	◉		◉		◉			
2. Dough is lumpy										◉	
3. Dough is too stiff		◉	◉	◉					◉		
4. Crust forms on rising dough											
5. Crust is too thick			◉								
6. Crust has separated from loaf							◉				
7. Baked loaf crumbles easily			◉								
8. Bread tastes sour							◉				
9. Bread has dark streaks											◉
10. Bread has holes in it					◉						
11. Bread is doughy on bottom			◉								
12. Bread has large break on side			◉	◉							
13. Bread doesn't rise in oven						◉	◉				
14. Bread is heavy and compact *	◉	◉	◉	◉		◉	◉	◉			
15. Bread is dry and coarse grained			◉	◉							
16. Bread falls in oven					◉	◉	◉	◉			
17. Bread doesn't brown							◉				
18. Bread smells and tastes yeasty					◉	◉	◉				
19. Bread comes out too flat			◉	◉	◉	◉	◉				
20. Bread lacks flavor				◉		◉				◉	
21. Tops of loaves are cracked			◉								
22. Bread is burned on bottom											

* Note this can result from letting dough rise too long or not long enough.
** The liquid may be too hot or too cold – should be about 110 degrees.
*** This is especially true if using powdered milk.

#	Dough not mixed well or evenly	Dough not kneaded well or evenly	Dough rose too long during 1st rise	Dough rose too long during 2nd rise	Dough rose too quickly	Dough didn't rise long enough	Dough not covered properly during rising	Rising place too cool or drafty ****	Rising place too warm	Dough not shaped properly	Dough shaped on floured board	Loaves were not slit before baking	Pans placed too close together	Shiny pans reflect heat away from dough	Pans too thin	Oven temperature too low	Oven temperature too high	Oven leaky or poorly insulated	Not enough steam in oven	Bread not baked long enough *****	Bread cooled too rapidly (draft?)
1.	●	●					●														
2.	●	●																			
3.						●															
4.			●			●															
5.					●											●					
6.						●						●				●					
7.	●	●	●	●			●									●					
8.		●	●	●			●														
9.	●	●					●			●											
10.	●	●		●		●															
11.			●											●						●	
12.					●						●						●	●	●		
13.		●	●				●														
14.	●	●		●		●															
15.	●	●	●		●	●										●					
16.			●	●			●														
17.																●	●	●		●	
18.			●	●	●		●														
19.		●																			
20.			●																		
21.	●	●					●														●
22.																●	●	●		●	

**** Your dough will rise in a cool place, but it will take longer
***** See *Rules of Thumb* on pages 19 & 20 in the "Tips and Techniques" section

To learn more about
Betsy Oppenneer and
where she is teaching,
visit her website at
www.breadworksinc.com
or
call The Breadworks, Inc.
603~632~9171

Index

8-Inch Whisk   13
10-Grain Dinner Rolls   114
10-Grain Mix   77
10-Grain Orange Bread   76
Active Dry Yeast (in bread)   16
Alfalfa Sprouts (in bread)   19
All-Purpose Flour (in bread)   17
Anadama Bread   78
Anise Orange Nut Rye Bread   84
Apple Cider Cinnamon Cloverleaf
   Rolls   102
Bagels   110
Baguettes
   Buttermilk Rye   90
   Garlic   36
   Gruyere   38
   Semolina Cheese   50
Baking Sheets   12
Baking Stone   12
Banana Bran Bread   80
Barley (in bread)   19
Basic White Learning Loaf   28
Batter, Tomato Cheese Bread   148
Bavarian Nussstollen   154
Beer Rye Bread   86
Bench Scrapers (Metal)   14
Berries, Wheat (in bread)   19
Black Peasant Bread   88
Bleached Flour (in bread)   17
Bowls, Ceramic   13
Braided Breads
   Braided Fruit Wreath   156
   County Fair Egg Bread   34
   Scandinavian Coffee Braid   170
Braided Fruit Wreath   156
Bran (in bread)   19
Bread Flour (in bread)   17
Bread Knives   15
Bread Pans   12
Breadsticks, Millet   134
Breadsticks, Nutty   132
Brioche   124
Brioche (Individual)   125
Brioche Pans   12
Brioche Cinnamon Rolls   126
Brown Sugar (in bread)   18
Brushes, Pastry   14
Buckwheat (in bread)   19
Bundt Pan   12

Buns, Wheat Berry   112
Butter (in bread)   19
Butterkuchen, German   160
Buttermilk Breads
   Buttermilk Orange Wheat Bread 62
   Buttermilk Rye Baguettes   90
   Honey Curry Bread   42
Buttermilk Orange Wheat Bread   62
Buttermilk Rye Baguettes   90
Calzone, Veggie & Sausage   150
Cane Syrup (in bread)   18
Caraway Rye Bread   92
Carrot Ginger Bread   30
Ceramic Bowls   13
Cheese Breads
   Chonion Pepper Bread   32
   Cottage Cheese Stollen   176
   Ensaymadas   104
   Focaccia, Mozzarella   129
   Focaccia, Provolone   128
   Gruyere Baguettes   38
   Parmesan Pita Bread   143
   Parmesan Potato Bread   54
   Provolone Focaccia   128
   Pull-Apart Bread (Savory)   58
   Semolina Cheese Baguettes   50
   Sesame Cheddar Bread   60
   Tomato Cheese Batter Bread 148
Chewy Oatmeal Bread   70
Chonion Pepper Bread   32
Cinnamon Raisin Pumpernickel
   Bread   94
Cinnamon Rolls
   Apple Cider Cinnamon Cloverleaf
      Rolls   102
   Brioche   126
   Sin-Amen Rolls   172
   Whole Wheat Cinnamon Rum
      Rolls   174
Cloverleaf, Apple Cider Cinnamon
   Rolls   102
Coconut Sunflower Seed Wheat
   Loaf   64
Compressed Yeast (in bread)   16
Cooling Racks   13
Corn Syrup (in bread)   18
Cottage Cheese Stollen   176
County Fair Egg Bread   34
Cracked Wheat   19

Cracked Wheat Breads
  Buttermilk Orange Wheat Bread 62
  Coconut Sunflower Seed Wheat
    Bread 64
  Cracked Wheat Bread 66
  Hearty Healthy Bread 82
Cracked Wheat Bread 66
Crusty Semolina Rolls 116
Cups, Measuring 14
Cynthia's Spudnuts 158
Danish Dough Whisk 13
Doughnuts, Cynthia's Spudnuts 158
Easter Twist, Greek 162
Eggs (in bread) 19
Ensaymadas 104
Fast-Rising Yeast 17
Fat (in bread) 19
  Butter 19
  Lard 19
  Margarine 19
  Oil 19
  Shortening, Vegetable 19
Flat Bread, Oriental 138
Flour (in bread)
  All-Purpose 17
  Bleached 17
  Bread 17
  Rye 18
  Soft Wheat 18
  Specialty 18
  Unbleached 18
  Whole Wheat 18
Fresh Yeast (in bread) 16
Fry Bread, Indian 140
Focaccia 127
  Garlic 129
  Herbed 128
  Mozzarella 129
  Olive 129
  Poppy Seed 128
  Potato 130
  Provolone Cheese 128
  Sesame Seed 128
Garlic Baguettes 36
Germ, wheat (in bread) 19
German Butterkuchen 160
Granulated Sugar (in bread) 18
Greek Easter Twist 162
Greek Pizza 147
Groats (in bread) 19
Gruyere Baguettes 38
Gugelhopf 164

Hearty Healthy Loaf 82
Heavy-Duty Mixer 16
Herb Bread 40
Herbed Focaccia 128
Honey (in bread) 18
Honey Curry Bread 42
How to Bake in a La Cloche 45
Indian Fry Bread 140
Individual Broiche 125
Instant-Read Thermometers 13
Italian Bread 44
Kneading Bread 20
Knives, Bread 15
Knives, Serrated 15
Knives, Tomato 15
Knotted Onion Sage Rolls 106
LaCloche, How to Use 45
Lard (in bread) 19
Learning Loaf, Basic White 28
Liquids (in breads)
  Beer 18
  Buttermilk 18
  Fruit Juice 18
  Milk 18
  Potato Water 18
  Sour Cream 18
  Vegetable Juice 18
  Vegetables, Puréed 18
  Water 18
Loaves
  10-Grain Orange Bread 76
  Anadama Bread 78
  Anise Orange Nut Rye Bread 84
  Banana Bran Bread 80
  Basic White Learning Loaf 28
  Beer Rye Bread 86
  Black Peasant Bread 88
  Buttermilk Orange Wheat Bread 62
  Buttermilk Rye Baguettes 90
  Caraway Rye Bread 92
  Carrot Ginger Bread 30
  Chewy Oatmeal Bread 70
  Chonion Pepper Bread 32
  Cinnamon Raisin Pumpernickel
    Bread 32
  Coconut Sunflower Seed Wheat
    Loaf 64
  County Fair Egg Bread 34
  Cracked Wheat Bread 66
  Garlic Baguettes 36
  Gruyere Baguettes 38
  Hearty Healthy Loaf 82

Herb Bread 40
Honey Curry Bread 42
Italian Bread 44
Maple Wheat Berry Bread 68
Mustard Seed Rye Bread 96
Parmesan Potato Bread 54
Pull-Apart Bread (Sweet) 58
Pull-Apart Bread (Savory) 58
Rosemary Raisin Bread 52
Semolina Cheese Baguettes 50
Semolina Olive Bread 47
Sesame Cheddar Bread 60
Sundried Tomato & Caramelized
    Onion Bread 56
Whole Wheat Raisin Nut Bread 72
Whole Wheat Seed Bread 74
Malt(ed) Barley Syrup (in bread) 18
Maple Cornmeal Rolls 118
Maple Syrup (in bread) 18
Maple Wheat Berry Bread 68
Margarine (in bread) 19
Measuring Cups 14
Measuring Spoons 14
Metal Bench Scrapers 14
Mixer, Heavy-Duty 16
Millet (in bread) 19
Millet Breadsticks 134
Millet Skillet Bread 136
Mincemeat Orange Rolls 166
Molasses (in bread) 18
Mung Bean Sprouts (in bread) 19
Mustard Seed Rye Bread 96
No-Knead Parkerhouse Rolls 100
Nutty Breadsticks 132
Oats (in bread) 19
Oatmeal, Chewy Bread 70
Oil (in bread) 19
Olive Focaccia 129
Onion Poppy Seed Rolls 108
Onion Sage Rolls (Knotted) 106
Oriental Flat Bread 138
Panettone 168
Pans, Bread 12
Pans, Brioche 12
Pans, Gugelhopf 12
Parchment Paper 14
Parkerhouse, No-Knead Rolls 100
Parmesan Pita Bread 143
Parmesan Potato Bread 54
Pastry Brushes 14
Pita Bread 142
Pita Bread, Parmesan 143

Pita Bread, Poppy Seed 143
Pita Bread, Sesame 143
Pita Bread, Whole Wheat 143
Pizza 144
Pizza Dough 144
Pizza, Greek 147
Pizza Sauce 146
Pizza Toppings 146
Plastic Dough Scrapers 14
Plastic Wrap 15
Poppy Seed Focaccia 128
Poppy Seed Pita 143
Potato Focaccia 130
Potato Water (in bread) 18
Powdered Sugar 18
Provolone Focaccia 128
Pull-Apart Bread (Sweet) 58
Pull-Apart Bread (Savory) 58
Pumpernickel Cinnamon Raisin
    Bread 94
Quick-Rising Yeast (in bread) 17
Racks, Cooling 13
Raisin Breads
    Cinnamon Raisin Pumpernickel
        Bread 94
    Rosemary Raisin Bread 52
    Whole Wheat Raisin Nut Bread 72
Rice (in bread) 19
Rolling Pin 15
Rolls (Savory)
    10-Grain Dinner Rolls 114
    Apple Cider Cinnamon Cloverleaf
        Rolls 102
    Bagels 110
    Crusty Semolina Rolls 116
    Ensaymadas 104
    Knotted Onion Sage Rolls 106
    Maple Cornmeal Rolls 118
    No-Knead Parkerhouse Rolls 100
    Onion Poppy Seed Rolls 108
    Parkerhouse, No-Knead Rolls 100
    Wheat Berry Buns 112
    Wheat Germ 'n Honey Rolls 120
Rolls (Sweet)
    Brioche Cinnamon Rolls 126
    Mincemeat Orange Rolls 166
    Sin-Amen Rolls 172
    Whole Wheat Cinnamon Rum
        Rolls 174
Rosemary Raisin Bread 52
Roux Whisks 13

Rye Breads:
  Anise Orange Nut Rye Bread 84
  Beer Rye Bread 86
  Black Peasant Bread 88
  Buttermilk Rye Baguettes 90
  Caraway Rye Bread 92
  Cinnamon Raisin Pumpernickel
    Bread 94
  Mustard Seed Rye Bread 96
Rye Flour (in bread) 18
Salt (in bread) 19
Sauce, Pizza 146
Scandinavian Coffee Braid 170
Scissors 14
Scrapers, Metal Bench 14
Scrapers, Plastic Dough 14
Semolina Breads
  Crusty Semolina Rolls 116
  Semolina Cheese Baguettes 50
  Semolina Olive Bread 47
Semolina Cheese Baguettes 50
Semolina Olive Bread 47
Serrated Knives 15
Sesame Cheddar Bread 60
Sesame Focaccia 128
Sesame Pita Bread 143
Shaping Dough 22
Shortening (in bread) 19
Sin-Amen Rolls 172
Skillet, Millet Bread 136
Soft Wheat Flour (in bread) 18
Sources 182-183
Soy Flour (in bread) 19
Specialty Flours (in bread) 18
Sponge Breads – See Starter Breads
Spoons, Measuring 14
Sprouts (in bread) 19
Starter Breads
  County Fair Egg Bread 34
  Cracked Wheat Bread 66
  Semolina Olive Bread 47
Stollen, Cottage Cheese 176
Stone, Baking 12
Storing Bread 24
Sugar (in bread)
  Brown 18
  Granulated 18
  Powdered 18
Sundried Tomato & Caramelized
  Onion Bread 56

Sweet Breads
  Bavarian Nussstollen 154
  Braided Fruit Wreath 156
  Brioche Cinnamon Rolls 126
  Cottage Cheese Stollen 176
  Cynthia's Spudnuts 158
  German Butterkuchen 160
  Greek Easter Twist 162
  Gugelhopf 164
  Mincemeat Orange Rolls 166
  Panettone 168
  Pull-Apart Bread 58
  Scandinavian Coffee Braid 170
  Sin-Amen Rolls 172
  Whole Wheat Cinnamon Rum
    Rolls 174
Sweeteners (in bread)
  Cane Syrup 18
  Corn Syrup 18
  Honey 18
  Malt(ed) Barley 18
  Maple Syrup 18
  Molasses 18
  Sugar, Brown 18
  Sugar, Granulated 18
  Sugar, Powdered 18
Syrup (in bread)
  Cane Syrup 18
  Corn Syrup 18
  Malt(ed) Barley 18
  Maple Syrup 18
Thermometers, Instant-Read 13
Tightly Woven Towels 15
Timer, Triple 15
Tomato Cheese Batter Bread 148
Tomato Knives 15
Towels, Tightly Woven 15
Triple Timer 15
Trouble Shooting 180
Unbleached Flour (in bread) 17
Utensils
  Baking Sheets 12
  Baking Stone 12
  Bench Scrapers (Metal) 14
  Bowls, Ceramic 13
  Bread Knives 15
  Bread Pans 12
  Brioche Pans 12
  Brushes, Pastry 14
  Bundt Pan 12
  Ceramic Bowls 13
  Cooling Racks 13

Index

Utensils Continued
  Cups, Measuring 14
  Gugelhopf Pan 12
  Heavy-Duty Mixer 16
  Instant-Read Thermometers 13
  Knives, Bread 15
  Knives, Serrated 15
  Knives, Tomato 15
  Measuring Cups 14
  Measuring Spoons 14
  Metal Bench Scrapers 14
  Mixer, Heavy-Duty 16
  Pans, Bread 12
  Pans, Brioche 12
  Pans, Gugelhopf 12
  Parchment Paper 14
  Pastry Brushes 14
  Plastic Dough Scrapers 14
  Plastic Wrap 15
  Racks, Cooling 13
  Rolling Pin 15
  Scissors 14
  Scrapers, Metal Bench 14
  Scrapers, Plastic Dough 14
  Serrated Knives 15
  Spoons, Measuring 14
  Stone, Baking 12
  Thermometers, Instant-Read 13
  Tightly Woven Towels 15
  Timer, Triple 15
  Tomato Knives 15
  Towels, Tightly Woven 15
  Triple Timer 15
  Whisk, 8-inch 13
  Whisk, Danish 13
  Whisk, Roux 13
Veggie & Sausage Calzone 150
Wheat Berries (in bread) 19
Wheat Berry Buns 112
Wheat, Cracked (in bread) 19
Wheat Germ (in bread) 19
Wheat Germ 'n Honey Rolls 112
Whisk, 8-inch 13
Whisk, Danish 13
Whisk, Roux 13

Whole Wheat Breads
  Buttermilk Orange Wheat Bread 62
  Chewy Oatmeal Bread 70
  Cinnamon Raisin Pumpernickel
    Bread 94
  Focaccia 127, 130
  Wheat Berry Buns 112
  Whole Wheat Cinnamon Rum
    Rolls 174
  Whole Wheat Pita Bread 143
  Whole Wheat Raisin Nut Bread 72
  Whole Wheat Seed Bread 74
Whole Wheat Cinnamon Rum
  Rolls 174
Whole Wheat Flour (in bread) 18
Whole Wheat Pita Bread 143
Whole Wheat Raisin Nut Bread 72
Whole Wheat Seed Bread 74
Yeast (in bread)
  Active Dry 16
  Compressed 16
  Fast-Rising 17
  Fresh 16
  Quick Rise 17

About The Author

Betsy Oppenneer's love of baking began when she was twelve years old while working in a bakery in Cleveland, Georgia. Since that time baking and cooking have become her true passion. She travels around the country teaching classes and sharing her love of food.

She is the author of *Betsy's Breads, The Bread Book, The Oppenneer Family Cookbook*, and producer of two videos on bread baking, *"Perfect Bread: How to Conquer Bread Baking"* and *"Perfect Bread: Fun with Creative Shapes."* Betsy currently writes a bi-monthly food-oriented newsletter, *From Betsy's Kitchen.* She lives in New Hampshire with her husband, Keith, and their three longhaired dachshunds, Clyde, Reba, and Traudl.